AF323528

COMMENTS

CONCEPTS
&
CONCLUSIONS

*Moving Toward a Final Point
of Understanding and Discovery*

by

Karl Pohlhaus

Fogfree

cover by Tim Broumley

edited by Karl Pohlhaus

ALL RIGHTS RESERVED

No part of this book may be reproduced in any form without permission in writing from the publisher, except by a reviewer who may quote brief pages for review purposes.

Hard cover edition
ISBN NUMBER: 0-9770301-3-X

TABLE OF CONTENTS

INTRODUCTION

This book has been entitled: Comments, Concepts and Conclusions because that is how ideas are formed. You start with comments. Comments, either written or spoken, that rise to the level of coherent ideas, create concepts. Concepts that rise to the level of conclusions provide others an opportunity to disagree or agree with those conclusions. As comments, one can agree or disagree as well, but comments by themselves remain solitary. The public Media can pick them up if spoken by someone considered important. But without foundation, they merely reflect the word of that someone. When they rise to becoming a concept, those comments now hold a cohesive quality. A pattern of ideas that demonstrate cohesion cries for attention. Concepts that stand up historically can begin their process of general acceptance with drawn conclusions based on evidence, data, results, and criteria that stand alone and apart from being ignored and forgotten.

The conclusions drawn in this text, from old and newly resurrected concepts, address what the author considers both important and relevant. Though the chapters appear to be randomly assigned, they all speak to basic notions of human beliefs. Most people are religious in one sense or another. How one conceives of God, Man and life becomes relevant to those many people because it informs them how to act and what to anticipate. Social organizations are informed by what we consider relevant, important and valuable. If things are considered more important than people, the political component of social organization will reflect that. How social organizations respond to their mandate reflect what they implicitly regard important. In our society, money has taken on an excessive importance to the detriment of people.

About the author

Karl who is known as Charlie, hails from Philadelphia. He went to a High School that gave him a B.A. degree upon graduation. After High School he went to a top Engineering College in Philadelphia, graduating with a B.S. degree, From here he attended a top Lutheran Seminary in Gettysburg, PA. Upon graduation and a short period in Lutheran ministry, Charles went back to Graduate School for another four years for yet another graduate degree in World Religions. With no specific plans for ministry, Charles once more became an Engineer working as a Planning Engineer for Catalytic, Inc.

Along the way Charles developed a keen interest in the nature of reality, both from a scientific perspective and a religious understanding. In time, Charles felt the call to journey West to San Francisco where he became friends with top Physicists. From here he came to Arizona to finally settle down with his wife of many years and once more enter ministry. This time he was called to a Brethren Church where he faithfully served for nine years before retiring. With retirement from ministry, Charles finally used his graduate degrees to teach Religion at both Glendale Community College in Glendale and Northern Arizona University extension in Phoenix, Arizona. It was in this setting, Charles finally began writing books reflecting his conclusions about reality and religions.

He brings to his books years of study, reflection and discussion with top people in their fields, mentors whose encouragement have prompted him to continue writing. A note of idealism marks his works along with a desire to see the world realize human potential and peaceful resolutions. to social issues.

The CHURCH and SCRIPTURE

One of Christianity's favorite passages from the Gospel of John is Jesus referring to himself as Being the Way, the Truth and the Life. Jesus goes on to say, "No one comes to the Father, but by me." Traditionally, the church has held such passages to mean that Jesus stands in a unique position among all other human beings as gatekeeper to God. Prior to the Reformation, the church pronounced itself as the gatekeeper to God and a blissful eternity. By the 6th century CE the church further saw the Bishop of Rome in a unique position as gatekeeper for all Christians. Jesus had given the keys of heaven and hell to Peter following Peter's pronouncement. Peter had affirmed that Jesus was the Christ, the Son of the living God. That pronouncement had prompted Jesus to grant on Peter the unique responsibility of gatekeeper for both heaven and hell. Now that same responsibility fell to the Bishop of Rome who would from this point on be known as the holy Father, Pope to all Catholics.

It is not difficult to see how Christian leaders could arrive at this conclusion. Peter has the keys. Those who follow him must also have the keys. Those who follow Peter also follow Jesus who has announced himself to be the door through which people can come into God's kingdom. Logic follows that the door is the only way in. Thus, Jesus is the only way into God's eternal kingdom. Latin Roman logic then would add that the church, through its head, would be the door to heaven.

Using Latin grammar and church logic leads to theology. Christian theology is Latin logic based on scriptural references carried forward through creeds, doctrinal statements and learned church lawyers. After the Reformation, theology would be placed in the hands of denominational scholars loyal to those unique emphases characterizing that Protestant church. Lutheran, Anglican and Reformed theologians would be the first, post Reformation, to write out theological statements for their church to use. Pastors would further those positions from pulpits, predigested for not as well educated lay people to reflect upon. These statements defined the faith, and thus were the clergy's and laity's path to God and heaven.

The passage previously referred to was generally accepted to mean what the Apostolic Fathers said it meant. The Protestants, now free to read the same passage and bible for themselves, moved the door away from the church and Pope to the Jesus of history and the only accepted text where one could find this Jesus. Salvation through this door was now not through an institution but through a matrix of theological faith statements believed and practiced. The bible was always a bedrock of the church. In Roman and Orthodox systems it stood with the creeds and traditional statements of the church. Most Protestant groups didn't question the creeds and early faith positions. They questioned the authority of the Roman church to see itself as the only door. It was a matter of authority. Rome rested its authority in itself. The many churches that rose out of the Reformation rested authority in the New Testament.

It wasn't until the 20th century that mostly Protestant scholars would question the text itself. Old Testament scholars looked at the Tanakh. Creation accounts interested them. Was there archeological evidence for the Genesis accounts. Both Christian and Reformed Jewish scholars noticed that the names for God were related to their origins. Historic evidence could trace the word Elohim to the divided kingdom of Israel before its destruction by the Assyrians. The four consonants of "Y", "H", "W", "H" were used by the Judah sources for the Holy Name of God. It proved to be holy because you could not pronounce YHWH. This was the secret name God had told Moses but not to be repeated by any but the high priest. Later upon the destruction of Jerusalem, it was forgotten.

*Other names for God appear in the Hebrew text. The oldest is **"EL."** Research uncovered that this oldest name for God was appropriated by the priests who sided with the newly formed kingdom of Israel. Israel needed to stand out from Judah and its temple in Jerusalem. It took the oldest name and added to it making the original masculine name "EL" both masculine, feminine and plural. Thus, "Elohim" became Israel's answer to the secret name residing in Jerusalem. Studying Genesis, scholars found both Elohim and YHWH early on in Genesis. Thus, the text revealed that at some point scholars in Judah had acquired the Israel material before it was lost and included it with their own creation stories. Likely the editing was done in Babylon during the almost 50 years the Jews from Jerusalem were in captivity.*

These three names form the basis of Jewish scriptures and worship. There are a number of descriptive titles that can substitute for the word God. Titles such as El Shaddai or God Almighty, the God of the high places, is descriptively duplicated by other titles a number of times. It was also noticed that the passage that contained Elohim also described a farming community in distinction to the passage that contained YHWH. Where YHWH was used the setting reflected a pastoral community raising sheep and goats. It was also noticed that such stories as Cain and Abel reflected Judah's dominance over Israel. The story of Cain and Abel appears after Israel's destruction. Cain sacrifices grain to please God. Abel sacrifices a sheep. One is a grain offering: the other a blood offering. The blood offering is more pleasing to this God. Thus, while grain offerings were used for the great temple in Jerusalem, blood offerings were more pleasing and more expensive to buy.

Location means a lot, wherever you live in the world. That was true of the Jews during the divided kingdoms of Israel and Judah. Israel was a good place to grow wheat. It was also relatively flat and good for chariots to speed through. Judah was hilly and good for raising livestock. Yet Bethlehem, which means House of Bread in Hebrew, was next to Jerusalem. A good location for raising sheep for temple sacrifice and production of bread. Roaming armies from Assyria and Egypt saw one another's empires as fruit to be picked. What appeared in front of their ambitions was Israel, the thoroughfare blocking their ambitions.

By the time of the Second Century CE, the church was comprised primarily of Gentiles who faced a daunting Rome bent on their destruction. Some time in the early CE period Roman emperors began calling themselves God. Some of the early ones to do so may have even believed they were gods. They had absolute power, a mighty empire at their disposal, the ability to pronounce any rules they wished and were comfortably settled behind guards loyal to their every whim. Christians, from those who had witnessed Jesus' resurrection, clearly did not agree with these pronouncements. They began calling Jesus Lord, not Caesar. A power struggle ensued that would end when Constantine became emperor. His rise to power would coincide with Christianity being accepted as the religion of the empire.

The Jews would be exiled from their homeland. In 70 CE Vespasian had ordered the troops to put down the rebellion in Israel. His troops were to eventually destroy the city and temple, killing or making slaves all Jews who they discovered. In 135 CE the remaining Jews who had filtered back to the remains of Jerusalem once more revolted against Rome. Led by a self proclaimed Messiah, they succeeded in killing the Roman garrison left there. Once more the Roman emperor, Hadrian, sent his troops to put down the rebellion. In efficient Roman style they killed or captured all Jews who opposed them. This time, Hadrian announced that any Jews who dared to remain in Israel would be killed. He renamed Israel, Palestine, a Roman name and invited none Jews to live there.

From the Second Century CE on, the Jews had no national identity. The Gentile Christians were now targets of Roman persecution. Christian scriptures were circulated among Christians following the Apostolic group, who had organized themselves around bishops chosen for their strength of faith and spirituality. These bishops believed they were the successors of the apostles from whom some of them had gotten the accounts of Jesus. There were other Christian groups, later to be known as Gnostics, who gathered different scriptures and followed a different style of teachings. The Apostolic party was more visible to Rome than their Gnostic cousins and so became easy targets for Roman persecution. Their overall bravery in the face of often painful deaths, won the respect of many rank and file Romans who honored bravery. Many converted to the Christian Apostolic faith because of the brave manner many of them died.

The scriptures the Apostolic party used comprised original documents, letters of the apostles and stories passed along. These were edited by Apostolic Christians as they copied them to be read in fellowships secretly meeting throughout the empire. In the First Century CE the Trinity did not exist, though Evangelical Christian scholars believe it did. Other Christian scholars point out that passages such as the last verse of Matthew were added by a zealous scribe who had no compunction having Jesus send his followers into all the world baptizing in the name of the Father, Son and Holy Spirit. That did not happen. It was likely added centuries later. Jesus never indicated he was equal to the God of Israel.

The first Jewish Christians believed Jesus was the authentic Messiah among a pool of many candidates. That was because many of them saw him after he was supposed to be dead. Messiah means "anointed." Those who had not witnessed him alive believed those who said they saw him. The sincerity of the eye witnesses and their bold manner in the face of both Roman and Temple authority persuaded the growing handful that something special had happened, a miracle of incredible dimensions. But they also said that God had raised Jesus out of death. He did not do it from his own power. These original Jewish Christians thought of Jesus as the one who would redeem Israel. They spoke of the several predictions in the Tanakh that foretold of a Messiah. The Gospel writer, Matthew, organizes his Good News around Jesus as the Messiah foretold by the prophets. But Jesus did not exactly fit the mold for many Jews. The Messiah was to either come from the line of King David and be a warrior king or he was to come from the line of Arron and be a spiritual priest.

The writer of Hebrews would paint Jesus as High Priest. Matthew would paint him as a king coming out of David's seed. He didn't really fit either according to Jewish expectations, but for those early Christians that didn't matter. He was alive and beyond Roman authority. He was, in fact, the new authority. The early Christians called him Lord. From Lord he would graduate to Christ, a Greek understanding of Messiah, but not the one predicated on Jewish expectations. Rather, he would become the cosmic Christ of the Gentiles.

Other letters and documents coming out of those early centuries continued to be circulated and edited by Christians running from Roman empirical authorities. The Gospel accounts describe Jesus as a healer, teacher, and prophet in the tradition of the Hebrew prophets before him. He did not side with the priests or power structure of his day. Average people heard him gladly and even wanted to just touch him. His popularity got the attention of the Romans. Roman authority in Jerusalem knew what he was doing, where he was and who came to hear him speak. When he got to Jerusalem for the last time, the Romans were ready to arrest him and crucify him for disturbing the peace of Rome.

The scriptures record a slightly different version, depending on which Gospel you read. Luke is Roman friendly and so paints Pilot as a fair administrator who is caught in the middle between rowdy Sadducees and disappointed radicals. Considering the Gospels accepted into the cannon, that following some time after the actual events in a climate of continued Roman hostility, it shouldn't be surprising that the Jews appear to be the ones to arrest Jesus, try him and finally submit a request to Pilot that he be executed. It is no accident the chief priest considers it better one man die than the entire nation perish. Pilot had his own secret police and informers. He had already crucified thousands of social revolutionaries. Jesus was a trouble maker who had to go if there would be peace in this region; a region he didn't enjoy administrating. He had no love for the Jews or their funny obsessions.

By the Third Century CE, the letters and Gospels, along with the special account written to Theophilus on the goings on of the First church and its mission, The Acts of the Apostle, were in circulation. The Apostolic Christians were convinced Jesus was more than a prophet, more than a Jewish Messiah, he was the only Son of the eternal God. Passages such as, "I and the Father are one," and "You are the Christ, the Son of the living God," and "In the beginning was the Word (Logos) and the Word was God," and than Paul's hellenized statements defined Jesus as the cosmic Christ, far above human identity. All of this conspired to give Jesus a unique identity unlike any Roman emperor, god, or potentate.

But Jesus was very human. He may have walked on water, but he credited anything he did to his Father and the permission his Father gave him. Jesus was humble to the point of even telling someone not to call him good, since only God Himself is good. That was an odd thing to say if he believed that he was uniquely God in human form. Certainly the Roman emperors had not exhibited humble qualities. But the church was convinced this Jesus was uniquely God and uniquely man, born of a virgin but capable of dying as a mortal being. The church, while beginning to distance itself from the Judaism that had born and nurtured it, saw their God as the same one who called the prophets, given the Torah to Moses, and promised father Abraham his descendants would be as numerous as the sands of the sea. This God was above the Roman gods. Jesus too, must be above them.

When you put yourself in that time, it becomes clear the early Apostolic Christians, once freed from Roman paganism and cruel Roman rulers, saw Jesus far above anything Rome or Greece could produce. He sat at the right hand of Almighty God, equal in nature, equal in power, equal in destiny. Humans were far beneath Jesus, mere rag-a-muffins in the presence of a divine King. That would insure his importance.

The strange thing about the final approval which came during Constantine's early reign at the Council of Nicea in 325 CE, is that Jesus never conducted himself as divine. He was just tuned in. Passages such as "I and the Father are one," could easily have meant that Jesus recognized who he belonged to and that he too was a spark of Divinity from this eternal flame of God. When Jesus taught his disciples to pray, he didn't say, "My Father who art in heaven," he said, "Our Father who art in heaven." Jesus called his disciples and probably many others, friend, not servant. He considered others as equals. That is why the people loved him. When a distinguished Rabbi relates intimately with unclean, polluted Jews and gentiles, that's news. Jesus' egalitarian attitudes and his popularity made him a threat to a Roman system that was top down, not bottom up. He was a mild threat to the self righteous Jews who had worked so hard to be separate from and better than most people. They were annoyed that Jesus appeared to be lowering the religious standards of his day. Actually, he wasn't doing that. He was advocating being in love with God and then obeying the laws God gave; God's voice put down in writing.

The Trinity as an authoritative doctrine, separates people from one another. It is another example of what Jesus was opposed to. It is Roman legality brought to the present time. The Trinity as symbolic reality invites, takes an inclusive view of God and humanity, and speaks volumes. Now, it places Jesus with his fellow men and with his beloved Father. Man becomes the bridge between two worlds when he recognizes his implicit divinity. Jesus recognized God as his real Father. He also recognized men and women as real brothers and sisters and taught that each should do the same. We have one real Father and many siblings of different colors, races, ethnic groupings and nationalities. The Trinity is the recognition that Jesus as prophet is transparent. He perfectly reveals the eternal God to others by standing as a bridge between heaven and earth: between God and Man. Totally human in every regard, he ate, slept, relieved himself, and suffered the indignity of death.

In ancient Israel the name for God, Elohim, revealed a masculine, feminine, and plural face, while the holy name of Judah was too holy to even speak. The Confucianists and Taoists in China understood that heaven, Tien, is masculine, or Yang. Earth is feminine, or Yin. The Tao itself is both indescribable void, yet everything that is. What could be more inclusive or egalitarian? In Judaism, the breath of God or His Spirit, is Ru'ah, a masculine noun. The presence of God, Shechinah is a feminine noun. The host of God is a collective plural and includes those who counsel him. God is singular and plural; beyond things yet in everything. Rather inclusive!

Jesus saw his mission as bringing all people to God, beginning with the House of Israel as self pronounced Messiah. His reward for being faithful to his calling was to return to the same Father who had sent him into this reality. Honors and accolades could be summed up in "This is my beloved Son in whom I am well pleased, listen to him." For Jesus, his role was clear. Reveal to those who would hear, that each was greater than he realized. Each was a spark of God in human dress. Each deserved to regard himself or herself in a more becoming manner and thus dress in a more becoming wedding outfit suitable for a wedding. Recognition prompts to action. Each should be prepared, by saving enough lamp fuel to be ready. All of the stories Jesus told, while focusing on different themes, were told to awaken in his hearers a God response.

Today they are often dissected to reveal ethical teachings or theological confirmations to support church doctrines. Jesus was certainly an ethical teacher and prophet. Jesus certainly confirmed the essence of the Torah and Talmud. But he never said or did anything to substantiate future doctrines and dogmas. He didn't come to focus on himself. He came to focus on God. That is why he remains transparent, as so many others have done or still do, who focus on God, giving God all the honor and glory. The early church, anxious to forever rid rulers of their arrogance of claiming to be God, did a great disservice to future generations. They placed Jesus in a unique role and identity as uniquely God / man. Jesus over emperor doesn't work. Emperor equal to all others, does.

The term "son of God" was rather common in Jesus' day. The children of Israel were thought of as sons of God. By making Jesus the unique Son of God, second person in the Trinity, the church pushed out the Jewish religion and all Jews. That was something Jesus would never have done. Following in the footsteps of Rabbi Hillel, Jesus put a humane face to a divinely revealed existing religion that was prone to becoming legalistic. What the church did was make it even more legalistic by making it doctrine based. The heart of any religion is experience. The heart of religious experience is Spirituality. The heart of Spirituality is Divine Presence, not formulations. The heart of all religions is ethical conduct. Ethical conduct is how you treat your neighbor, not how you stand out from your neighbor. It is the combination of ethical behavior and Spiritual presence that awakens our true identity as it did in Jesus, who practiced both ethical living and divine presence.

The Chinese have their own notion of Trinity. It is heaven, Tien or extreme Yang; earth, or extreme Yin; and Man who stands in the middle, infused with both Yin and Yang. Judaism is strictly monotheistic, yet recognizes a male and female presence of God. It is interesting that the male breath of God or Spirit has the same male quality that Heaven or air has for the Chinese. Air is active, comes as it wills, and can relieve or destroy. It is interesting that the female presence or Spirit of God has the same female quality that earth or nature has for the Chinese. Earth invites, provides and sustains humanity.

The prophetic message has its own trinitarian component, as pronounced by the prophet, Micah. God wants man to do Justice; love Mercy; and walk humbly with God. **Justice**, **Mercy**, *and* **Righteousness** *in action fulfills man's requirements. Righteousness is obeying God's voice as told by God's law. Compassion softens the heart and heals relations.*

More should be said about Justice since it is central to Judaism. At it core, Justice is treating everyone fairly and equally. That is not easy to do naturally since humans are prone to treat those they like with favor, from family, love ones and influential persons. Those who irritate, oppress and ignore us tend to be treated in like fashion. But for the believing Jew, Justice must be done or God is not honored and obeyed. The Talmud spells out one type of circumstance after another to clarify how Justice is to be met.

Treating everyone uniquely yet equally is difficult. It requires intention, discernment and honesty. A humble person is honest to the extreme, not because that person has little self esteem, but because he or she doesn't have more than is his or her due. Nor is it a matter of refusing to recognize the God within that makes one humble and honest. The greater the recognition of the divine spark, the more humanely and cooperatively a person behaves. Mystics attest to this phenomenon. It is the person with little real self esteem and much dishonesty, who convinces himself he is better than the other, and therefore has the right to use and abuse the other. That is not honesty or humility or divine recognition.

Compassion or mercy draws to others. Justice knows what to do once contact is made. Walking with God alerts us as to how to carry Compassion and Justice forward. All work together to help, not hurt humanity and creation and thus serve divine intention as that intention is internalized in the doer.

Opposites tend toward a third component for balance. Thus, extreme Yin and Yang as in Earth and Sky, is balanced by man in the middle. God as Breath (Ru'ah) and Presence (Shechinah) is balanced by humanity when humanity recognizes the Breath that gives it life now and eternally and the Presence that affirms Man as connected to the Eternal. Both Breath and Presence form the mystic experience and thus complete the ones so awakened. Doing Justice, loving Compassion and actively pursuing Righteousness accomplish the same thing from the outward reaching aspect of this inner experience.

The emperor in China went to a special place twice a year to invoke heaven and earth to bless the land through his person. When he was sincere and not ceremonial, heaven and earth drew into his person with both Yang and Yin, energizing and balancing him. When he saw his role as a divinely commissioned responsibility on behalf of his land and country, everyone benefitted.

When what the church bishops, acting on behalf of the Holy Roman emperor, instituted as legal law, the benefit was reversed and Christianity stood off against the other religions as superior and non-relational. When the day comes that the Trinity will be understood as mystical reality that will change.

*Religious reality is both Monism and Monotheism. Moving this reality to include man supplies the social dimension to a reality that needs to include man for spiritual evolution to move forward. In the **final** analysis there is only God who is everywhere the same. In the **temporal** analysis there is creation and God; everything that is, and the void that supports it. Intelligence is throughout and therefore consciousness is throughout. Consciousness at God's level has been called supra-consciousness. It can also be understood as non particular, universal consciousness, beyond this and that. At the creational level, consciousness is both aware and alert. Awareness is subconscious. Alertness is normal consciousness. Each plays it parts. Each is part of a whole fabric in much the same manner that the Divine is the whole fabric, delineated in infinite ways.*

So, while the church was anxious to nail down the experience of Jesus by endlessly defining his two natures and why the Trinity is the only way to express the revelation of God in Jesus the Christ, using Latin logic to accomplish these two preoccupations only furthered Rome's predilection for power over others. It did not seek to understand why one God was as valid as three in one God, and thus isolated the mother religion from her delinquent offspring. The problem would be compounded when Mohammed experienced his own revelation over 22 years. Islam would be called a pagan heresy worthy of killing and converting rather than honoring and understanding. The die was cast beginning in 325 CE at Nicea.

How one reads scriptures says much about the one reading. Literalistic readings may closely reflect an absolutistic personality who at some point became afraid to think or conclude by himself. Fear of being damned, and the prospect of eternal Hell may have driven him to simply accept the text as if it were dropped from heaven. Over time a sense of confidence that he was on the right side caused him to conclude others of a different view were outside his pale of concern or compassion. Those conclusions loosely resemble the Hindu Brahmin's attitude toward the lower castes who need to work out their karma themselves. No one can do it for them so why reach out to help or care. It's every man for himself. The same attitude may be observed in the Orthodox Jew or Christian who has convinced himself that he has all the truths needed to find salvation, so why run the risk of being polluted with a divergent view.

But in the case of a true Orthodox Jew the Talmud drives him to be righteous, and being righteous means more than observing proper ritual, it includes charity and mercy. In the case of the Orthodox Christian, charity is a part of his tradition, so observing it has a place. How much or how little is left to conscience. In the case of Fundamentalist Christians, more are discovering that social ethics was what Jesus was all about. Copying him compels that style of Christian to do charitable works, especially for foreign situations and global catastrophes. In the case of the liberally minded Christian the social Gospel is central, even if experience is not.

Catholic Christians have witnessed to religious experience throughout the last two thousand years of church history. Usually the experience comes while praying or meditating. It comes while in a state of worship. But it seldom has been reported while reading the bible. That is partly because the bible is one of two standards Roman Catholic and Orthodox Christians have. The other standard is the living tradition. For Rome that includes the first seven Ecumenical Councils, plus the subsequent councils that have come along.

For Protestant Christians, some sort of mystical experience comes by reading and meditating on the scriptures themselves. The Spirit appears to spring from the pages and Jesus speaks through the text. Full blown mysticism has befallen both Protestant and Catholic believers. When that happens it is far more than the acceptance felt when taken into full communion with that church body or after being born again. Full mysticism has been described by those who lay claim to it as being enveloped by the presence of God or Christ, and loosing track of time or boundaries. The mystic doesn't know where he or she ends and God begins. The experience is indescribable, yet having characteristics of absolute peace, love, joy and knowing. God becomes so real as to be immediate in presence and time. Mystics consider what happened to them as a mountain top moment. While wanting it to last forever, each one knows he or she must return to the valley and do the work the mystic has been assigned. Each one knows that moment will come again and last forever.

For those who have had real mystical experiences, defining Jesus as God or Son of God or eternally real are not important. In fact definitions, so important to Western thinkers, fall by the wayside. Time is an illusion. Eternity is now and always. The inability to differentiate between God and man addresses the core of the mystical union. Christian mystics have felt depression upon returning to ordinary life. Eastern mystics have not. Teachings of self depreciation have much to do with that. Eastern religious people anticipate something inside of them will recognize God, because that something is God related. A sense of parenthood is natural. In the moment, Christian mystics don't care about boundaries or their inadequate self. God is the all important factor and God completely accepts them as they are. Traditional beliefs attribute that to God's immense mercy. While true, the actual reason is because what is kin recognizes what is ultimately related. What is total love, compassion, truth, and power slips past what is self limiting and self creating to the true nature, pure and undefiled by life's experiences.

The First Century Jewish Ebionites believed in the resurrection of Jesus but not in his divinity. Constantine's Byzantine empire pushed them out. Arius, a presbyter of Alexandria, believed that Jesus was a human being subservient to God as Father. For Arius, Jesus was a created being. He issued from God at the beginning with a mission to fulfill. Arius was pushed out and finally lived out his life in exile. The Roman model was singularity; one faith, one theology.

Traveling briefly through the scriptures making comments along the way, leads to concepts and personal conclusions. Caring enough about what is true and real prompts concepts and subsequent conclusions. Adhering to doctrines and dogmas simply because others have accepted them is not enough. Modern scholarship knows the scriptures were edited over time before accepted as cannon. The social model of the Byzantine empire, Rome transplanted to Constantinople, was a top down system that prized uniformity, not experience. Rome of later centuries would follow that model with one exception. Instead of the emperor being the head of the church, the bishop of Rome would become the head of the Western church. Singularity would still stifle independent thought.

The biblical discoveries of the Ninetieth and Twentieth Centuries created, in one faction of the Christian community, the hint that proclamations decided in the Fourth Century CE may not reflect divine intention or real events. It doesn't matter if everyone needs to believe that Jesus is God in the second person. It does matter Jesus relates to those who want to relate to him God's eternal love and divine kinship. It does matter that believers know they have a right to be with God because they recognize God as their parent. For those who find it difficult to fathom trinities, they are more common than one might suppose. It may be more meaningful to understand that Jesus presents the face of God and Moses presents the voice of God. But both present God and both offer his eternal Presence.

BUREAUCRACIES

Bureaucracies have been on the scene for a very long time. They typically form the government of a country as well as its commercial infrastructure. It would be helpful to look back to their beginnings to gain some perspective as to why they are so pervasive today.

Bureaucracies express social form and organization. The earliest social forms were groups who huddled together for protection. The strongest member of this huddled group became their leader, first because he could beat out applicants, and second because he helped the group to survive and even thrive. In time, the leader became the tribal chief.

Leadership is more than human inspired. Higher forms of life, such as mammals for the most part, congregate in groups. Groups work better when they have a leader. Flocking birds fly with a leader in front. Dominant animals often lead herds of females or combinations of young males and submissive females. Solitary mammals are their own leaders and prefer not to socialize until mating season. Some humans prefer being solitary, but human beings are social creatures who crave intimacy. Where there are groups there are leaders. The organization of a group helps the group survive, move and even institutionalize itself into a permanent entity. Leadership helps the group accomplish its goals and expectations. Consequently, leaders have always been at the head of groups formed for a common purpose, beginning with simple survival.

Hunter/gathering societies moved with their food supply. They hunted game as it was available and gathered from the natural elements what they needed for shelter, sustenance and recreation. Hunters became adept at both finding and killing game. They became proficient at reading signs and following trails. They developed weapons for defense, killing and capturing what they needed. Over time their killing included fellow people who presented themselves as targets. Defenseless tribes whose land presented a desirable alternative also presented these hunter/gatherers an opportunity to rest from their constant travel and develop sources of labor saving alternatives for existing tribesmen. Slaves were born to societies that discovered their capability of obtaining human prisoners. It was more profitable to capture and condition humans and animals than to kill them. As captured humans and animals chose to cooperate they also chose to serve others.

Civilizations sprang from the combination of hunter/gatherer and planter societies. The Hunters took the role of overseer: the planters took the role of farmer and craftsman. The hunter learned to protect: the planter learned to supply. This seeming symbiotic relationship saw variations in different cultures. Intelligent, well cultured planter societies were able to forge more equal relations. In fact, the hunter elements often discovered themselves in a subservient role in the face of confidence producing, highly motivated non warrior types. It is no accident that the Brahmin caste considered itself over the warrior caste. It is no accident soldiers would serve rulers.

With the advent of Western civilizations, tribal chiefs were viewed as appointed by God to lead the people. This may have started with the coronation of Charlemagne, Chieftain of the Franks, a powerful tribal system in the Northern region of what is today France, Charlemagne considered himself more than a chief, he was King of the Franks. Over time, the various regions habitated by tribal groups became identified as nations. National identities, in part, could be characterized by language and interest. The Germanic tribes claimed Charlemagne as their own, calling him Karl the Great. Germanic language copied latin grammar while developing more guttural sounds. France took more words from the Latin but developed an easier grammar. Spain, Portugal and Italy did the same. Latin itself, would become relegated to Church and Law. So many different tribal systems had migrated through Italy, Spain and France looking for suitable land to call their own, these countries' languages would resemble Latin but be quite different. Defined language was to also define national identity.

Governments developed around the king and his court. Distinguished lords of the king would assume responsibility over territories. Barons, Dukes, etc. were granted land and position in keeping with their loyalty to the king and their ability to govern on behalf of the king. As the king's power waned so did that of his faithfully entrusted. Populations that were ruled on behalf of the king would now be governed by agencies and bureaus. Kings would be figureheads to be honored by history, while national agencies governed.

But how does a national agency or local bureau govern? The old style of leadership was always assumed to be superior to democratic decision making. After all, the Byzantium style of Roman rulership had worked well for the Roman empire from Constantine to the Fall of Constantinople. The Roman bishop system in Italy became the Papal system and would announce itself as the Holy Roman Empire in charge of Italy and then Northern Europe. It too, governed with top down style of leadership. It wasn't perfect, but was able to manage its affairs. With the advent of more socialistic styles of government, the introduction of Bureaucracies was inevitable. Bureaucracies were internal governments loyal to both leadership and the people governed. Leadership appointed bureau heads as kings had appointed Knights to govern sectional lands and people. But bureaucracies, for the most part, operated by national location and function, rather than kingly approval.

Russia had a strong bureaucratic structure in place while the Czar was in charge of the country. The country was too large to be effectively managed by loyal clan. China had developed Bureaucracies during the time of the first great dynasties. The Confucius model was put in place with Wo Ti, a wise emperor during the Han period. Chinese bureaucracies practiced an honorable system, primarily built on ability, human worth and emperor loyalty. People were served and the nation prospered. The emperor was served when the people had enough to eat, a place to call their own, and the ability to earn a living that benefited the nation as a whole.

As the power of Kings declined in Europe, the governments in Europe adopted the Socialistic model. Socialistic governments need bureaucracies to manage. The heads of these bureaucracies may be elected or chosen by the political government in power. Heads were known by the title of lord, a title previously reserved for the royal knights of the realm. England went so far as to have a House of Lords, a governing body of aristocratic men chosen from the original dukes and dignitaries whose claim to king and land went back centuries to another time. The House of Commons represents the common people and is reserved for elected representatives. This over all system assumes that educated gentlemen, of noble birth and bearing, can counterbalance the rough and uneducated rabble who insist on a seat of power.

In America, our country was founded by two streams of political will. The Constitution was written and approved by both philosophically minded statesmen. The one favored a branch of government that was educated, cultured and better able to dictate the complicated affairs of this new land. The other favored the philosophy of populists and social revolutionaries who felt strongly that given correct information, the people would choose the best course a country would travel with representatives wed to the greater good of the people and their will. National agencies were from the beginning, agencies of national services. With the Constitution ratified and working, bureaucratic agencies were and are essential to the proper operation of governmental services.

As the country grew and became more complex, additional agencies were added. It was inevitable that America would have as many agencies as any of the Socialistic governments of Europe, even though our form of government was different than the Parliamentary systems prevalent in Europe. Our commercial system of doing business grew with defining America as Capitalistic. Roots of this commercial driven system of buying and selling capital dovetailed the introduction of Wall Street, the invention of corporations and the Federal Reserve System that allowed the government to sell money at a low interest to Banks and Lending Agencies so that they, in turn, could loan that money at a higher rate of interest. This was quite similar to the money changing practices of the Sadducees in Biblical days prior to the destruction of the great Temple in 70 CE. In medieval times, Jews were not allowed to own land but could act as banks and loan money. Christians felt it was unchristian to do so in keeping with church practice.

Capitalism worked because of laws introduced to make money more accessible. But Capitalism only works if money flows. The value of money is directly related to its flow and its valuated guarantee by the Federal Government. The value of money appears to only move from greater to lesser. This appears to be a direct consequence of raising prices with greater demand. Since the intrinsic value of quality items and services remains the same, the charged cost for these items and services, depends on the demand associated with them. Scarcity consequently, effects costs along with demand.

Capitalism stands in contrast to Socialism, yet both deal with economic issues and both have outstanding economists in the service of their respective countries. Economists may have favorite areas of focus, but all are interested in goods and services that enhance a nation's health and well being. Economists tend to gravitate to one or another over arching theory, basing their predictions on their favorite theory. Our capitalistic system, as regulated by the Federal Reserve, tends to evaluate the health of the economy from accumulated assets rather than jobs held. The successful flow of money, profits and corporate growth appear to have greater merit than higher percentages of people employed in good paying positions and jobs, with reasonable hours that afford leisure and family time.

Productivity, a function of sales and profit, is directly related to efficient results and many hours at work. That is not only true with blue collar work but white collar work as well. Increased productivity needs a market of buyers. That market is maximized when price goes down with labor costs. The lower the labor costs or salaries with the maximum hours worked, the more profit the company or corporation makes and the more widgets it sells. But if the domestic market can't afford to buy the product it must either be sold internationally or payment plans devised that allows a domestic market to play. The car industry is a good example. The price of cars have steadily risen in sizable increments over the last fifty years from less than $1,500 per car to $25,000 per comparable car. Payment plans then allow the market to buy what is overpriced.

If the car market were actually a free enterprise market, a car manufacturer would have come along and introduced a vehicle considerably less expensive and of higher quality than what is presently available. That doesn't happen because this market is not a free market. Along with many other markets, this market is tightly regulated by a friendly federal government receptive to existing industry demands and influence, and an industry with vested interest in controlling what people are allowed to purchase.

There were cries arising from one side of the political aisle that big government that favored labor and welfare was ruining our national economy by giving away huge amounts of money for votes and regulating corporations to the point of strangulation. Like so many talking points, the large governmental welfare bureaucracies created to take care of people were inefficient, yet extremely practical when thinking heads realized that people who get welfare are able to buy products and services. On the other hand, the corporate welfare that has bailed out large corporations to live another day, has not realized a benefit related to the purchase of goods and services. Those heading up these corporations have realized huge profits and feathered their own nests from public funds, without the greater economy benefitting. Such is the position of political parties that favor corporate interests and wealthy backers, ahead of the rank and file citizens who comprise the greater majority of people. Such is the political position that began with Alexander Hamilton and still exists today.

Bureaucracies are inherently inefficient today as they have been. Like democracy, they act slowly waiting for some kind of invisible signal to move. What the one side of the aisle neglected to mention is that governments need them to function at all levels, local, state and national. It is no accident the federal governmental bureaucracies did not diminish during conservative regions; they increased. Bureaucracies are indispensable to the working of a large nation. They are indispensable to the working of a large corporation as well.

Talking heads have promoted the notion that turning over government agencies/bureaucracies to private companies will make them run more efficiently and more cheaply. That is not so, nor can it be so given the nature of managing a large operation. The only difference between continuing to have large government agencies manage as is, and turning them over to a privately funded group, is profit. Private companies and public corporations need to turn a profit. They do so, not by operating more efficiently, but by operating more cheaply, paying lower salaries, working people longer hours and raising prices and rates. Large banks, energy companies and industrial corporations make money by getting rid of competition through mergers. Once the merger is approved, the bank, company or corporation lays people off, saving salaries, and makes those still working, work longer. Mergers do exactly what conservative politicians have accused liberals of doing, eroding free enterprise based on free competition. Fewer and fewer companies exist, charging higher rates and prices.

That does not settle the issue of Bureaucracies. Why has no-one come forward with a new model of organization that would serve the public in a more useful and better manner? Using the term "efficient" may not add anything to "useful and better", so that term will be used in a limited manner. Social organizations may run more efficiently, when they run more smoothly, more easily, and more responsibly. With that understanding, the term "efficient" can resume an honorable place at the table of definitions. It should not mean running an organization more cheaply, because frankly, that means the labor force is doing more than they should for less income, and stock holders reap a higher return. Higher stock dividends do not mean the economy is doing well. Higher dividends means a few are doing well at the expense of many who aren't.

If we accept the concept that bureaucracies evolved from state governments with the decline of kings and nobles ruling their estates, we can also accept the concept that what makes bureaucracies function is their mandate from the leadership of the country. Thus, they are part of the top down social systems of times past, stretching back to the first hunter/planter societies that both roamed the land and settled in fertile regions. The leadership principles are still in effect, often to the detriment of those bureaucracies mandated to serve. Most National agencies hold the top position open for the incoming Political leader elected to lead the country. When his party controls Congress there is always the possibility that Congress and the President will alter the original mandate.

National Bureaucracies need to have leadership that remains in place, honoring the original mandate of the agency. Leadership of bureaucracies <u>should be</u> the direct result of internal democratic elections in which all employees can choose who will lead them. Safeguards <u>should be</u> put in place that make it impossible for top management to effect such elections by negative bullying or by positive incentive bribery. Implementing the directive of the agency <u>should be</u> the only criteria for achieving management status or titular head status. Mistakes in delivery of service, treatment of internal employees, and mismanagement of resources <u>should be</u> publicly admitted prior to a requested vote of confidence, and proposed remedy enacted, with assurance that the remedy is permanently in place. These "<u>should be</u>'s" insure a better bureaucracy.

Funding of the agency, once the agency is up and running, needs to be taken out of the hands of the funding source and regularly approved by a general election with all factors known, internally and externally. Partisan factions capable of manipulating an agency from the outside have a way of compromising even the best intentioned bureaucracy. As to a smooth and helpful ordering of business, often referred to as an efficient operation, the workers from the top, down to the bottom, can determine the best way to maximize production, allocation and communication of product and service, given all available information. Regular self checks will uncover better methods and requirements that an all employee meetings can resolve. The social organism is capable of correcting itself.

Several Republican presidents in the 1800's worked on objectifying Civil Service bureaucracies to insure their independent status. Their contribution greatly improved national service. It should be noted that the independence shown by these patriotic service minded presidents earned them a one term status. Their party did not put them forward for reelection. But their reforms are not enough, because the problem is systemic.

Companies are identified as bureaucracies when they reach a certain size. Corporations are also bureaucracies because, unlike smaller private companies, they have organized around directorships, department heads, vice-presidents and stockholders. That removes them from singular leadership decisions based on the right of owners to determine daily methods of running affairs. Corporations have a top down system that have introduced a host of auxiliary functions including marketing, legal affairs, procurement, expediting, sales forces and department managers. With the introduction of multiply tasks, the corporation must coordinate activities to optimize sales, profit and legal operations. In our system, profit becomes the primary consideration. But securing profit is now based on not exceeding costs, including salary packages and employee benefits. Pleasing stockholders and investors becomes an essential ingredient for growth and market share. Our system is based on free competition, but free competition soon becomes a word for public information, not reality once other competitors are eaten up and political interference is included.

The inherent weakness with promoting the notion that competition is better for a free economy is that it seldom exists. Only small companies competitively battle in a free system. The big players are able to buy their way out of a competitive market through political contributions, sellouts, hostile takeovers and undermining other players in the marketplace. The Law of the Jungle is the only rule by which large players operate. Greed trumps honesty and effort. Hidden ways of producing cheaper products complements raising prices to increase profit. Product reliability can easily be hidden under dollars of advertisements. Appearance always flanks reliability and without a vigilant governmental agency to monitor and prosecute cheating corporations, corporations can continue to deceive the public with inferior products and services long after those products and services have demonstrated their real worth. At some point the corporation will fail. The major players, will by this time have secured huge nest-eggs of capital and outside investments and abandoned the ship of corporate greed. The ones who suffer are always the employees who never had a voice in how to restore the integrity of the corporate bureaucracy.

This scenario plays itself out time and again, especially during political administrations that favor business and banks. These institutions consider it to be their birthright to place the burden on average taxpayers while stealing billions. The reason the rich get richer is because they can. The reason the poor get poorer is because they play by reasonable rules of conduct.

There will come a time when the general public will opt to elect political representatives who will change the way corporations are formed and continue. All bureaucracies, including public and private corporations, national and state and local agencies will run according to different standards of operation. But for this to happen talking heads, political candidates, and media not wed to commercial interests must collectively bring proposals to the public that include permanent changes to the structure and operation of bureaucracies wherever they are found.

What would a bureaucracy look like? First, the organization should be larger than a small business. Small businesses should be protected from unreasonable government regulations related to employees, benefits and salary scales. Once the company is large enough to be identified as a corporation or agency, than the opposite should be in effect. Large companies, corporations and agencies need to be democratically organized. Employees should be protected by rights of the work place, fair salaries in keeping with market profit or useful service to the public. All management and corporate heads should be chosen internally by the rank and file employees, not internally by boards or externally by political appointments. Once a company becomes a corporation or agency, it is owned by the general public and must serve the best interests of that public, not shareholders, vested interests or C.E.O.'s. Ombudsmen should be hired by each agency and corporation to police that corporation from the top down.

Corporations that sell products need to detail cost and quality through a general internal review open to all employees. Cost of product should not be the privilege of financial departments who will try to charge the highest price with the most advertising dollar. Advertisements need to change to only include description, materials and design efforts, not psychological ploys to buy or social ploys to belong. Quality needs to be such that the product is either described as a cheap throwaway or long lasting with great resale value regulated by age and not deception. The car Industry is not the only corporate industry that will reel from these legislated changes. The old joke about the honesty of Used Car Salesmen need to be put to rest in light of a limited market in which the buyer need not beware.

Today, automotive engineers are not hired to maximize quality and design, but planned obsolescence and higher parts replacement. Parts can be interchangeable for all automobiles if mandated to be so. Designs can be simpler to insure long life if mandated to be so. Self repair, a long lost right of car owners can be returned with cleaner burning engines if mandated by Federal will. That and more, is very possible when the will and truthfulness is there. It is easy to hire someone to discredit change on behalf of an Industry that controls the media and governmental agencies. It takes a vision and dedication to promote a view that will not allow fear of the future and loss of control to mandate what the public gets, in contrast to what the public deserves.

Governmental agencies are too important to be controlled by political parties. They need to be only answerable to the public they serve. Limiting the privileges of political representatives alters what our founding fathers had in mind, but they could not have envisioned the ability of politicians to hold so much power in so few hands as to make the representative form of government they hoped would endure act so poorly. The fault does not lie with the intrinsic structure of a bureaucracy, though that is flawed. The fault lies with the basic mandate of politics: power and control. When either side of the aisle controls what happens, one side may act more to favor the working man than the other, but both are beholden to financial vested interests that favor themselves at the expense of the greater public. As long as money runs politics, the average citizen is not heard or is he or she served.

The hunter personality favors the political party that believes that a few know what's best for the many. The ability to control and kill what opposes you fits the hunter personality that sees killing innocent game as it's birthright irregardless of the simple fact killed game is no longer needed to comfortably sustain life. Unlimited access to guns, which clearly helps the criminal element is envisioned as our birthright to the exclusion of good sense and fair rules. Prohibiting purchase of a firearm to anyone prior to a careful background check that may take weeks makes good sense. Limiting gun dealers to those who are not going to go for the dollar because they are salaried by the state, makes more sense than the profit driven current system.

Gun Manufacturers, whose lobby powers rival the Pharmaceutical companies, are all bureaucracies that require a new face and new personnel. Their influence with congressional representatives, statewide or nationwide should be zero. It far outweighs the public interest currently. Profit drives both industries to the point of endangering human life and should be treated as such. A new bureaucratic face would include zero lobbying dollars, independent executives from police, prosecutorial aide and scientific consultants whose expertise is able to access public safety. There is a saying that goes: "If you take the profit out of war, countries will not go to war." Where there is no advantage there is no war. The same is true of corporate bureaucracies that have taken over public markets.

There is nothing intrinsically wrong with making a living or enough money to have what you need or want. There is something intrinsically wrong with making so much money others are hurt by what you do or cause to happen. The market place is only one criteria for business. The more important criteria is service that enhances but does not harm others. What is true for gun manufacturers and Pharmaceutical corporations is also true of Police and Fire Departments and any departments, agencies and arms of the state or national government that have a specific mandate to serve the public good. Each should be independent, free of political will, and directly answerable to the general public whom they serve. Each should be able vote for their managers, department heads and acting head of that bureau, with veto ability.

Another way of accessing what bureaucracies need to be is the planter model of organization which is intrinsically egalitarian. The planter is dependent on a number of variables, including favorable weather and sincere effort. The planter works with nature, respects what is natural and works toward a bumper crop. The planter knows that peace works much better than warring against forces outside of his control, so he doesn't try to control. He tries to cooperate with nature. The planter personality is superior to the hunter personality, as the European socialist bureaus are superior to the profit driven capitalistic bureaucracies which dot our landscape. But even the socialistic models don't go far enough, even as the sterling efforts of those several Republican 19th century presidents did not go far enough to correct Civil Service.

Financial and organization independence is crucial, as is democratic internal decision making. Respecting the primary mandate for existence is important as are safeguards that review the bureaucracy's ability to honor its mandate. Public bureaus and agencies have a single overriding mandate of public service for all the public, not simply the privileged few. They have other mandates depending on their charter. Once given a charter, the agencies should be relatively independent to honor their mandate, free of political interference. If the political representatives believe the agency is out of control and has not reviewed and internally corrected any excesses, the public can vote on corrective action. All bureaucracies are beholden to the general public and regional public they serve.

The conclusion that all agencies and corporate bureaucracies be changed includes such agencies as the IRS. The IRS should have one overriding mandate: to collect taxes. That means to institute a graduated tax base that includes all corporate entities, even religious ones. A fair tax system would include the following: earnings of from zero dollars up to but not including $50,000 yearly earnings are tax free. From $50,000 up to $100,000 a tax liability of 10%. From $100,000 to one $1,000,000 , 20%. From $1,000,000 up to but not including $10,000,000, 30%. From $10,000,000 to but not including, $50,000,000, 40%. From $50,000,000 to but not including $100,000,000. 50%. Anything over $100,000,000, 50% maximum tax liability. No credits or exemptions allowed. Money invested would be taken from the income not taxable. Small churches, businesses and private persons will have little tax liability. Large churches, businesses and private persons will pay automatically with money taken out monthly. Tax returns should not include money but an acknowledgment or denial that this money was earned and money deducted.

Even though economists wed to either political party or large interests, would deny the viability of this graduated tax system, it could easily be proven that what this country needs could easily be paid without a growing national debt. The inability of Congress to live within its means is criminal. Therefore, Congress should not be given the right to alter this tax program. In fact, Congress should be mandated to continually pay down the debt and budget accordingly.

The criminal court system works, but often poorly. Wealthy persons and corporations have multiply lawyers who delay prosecution or make it extremely difficult to honor the law. Because we have a common law system based on a combination of statute and prior decisions, the law becomes based on legalities in contrast to justice. The financially strapped citizen often finds quick injustice while the financially gifted citizen drags out court proceedings until the judgment falls in his favor. Changing the laws to be simple and provable appears to be essential. Taking the money out of legal proceedings will help that along. Quick decisions, with quick appeals, is also essential. When all parties have done their best to prove innocence or guilt, the sentence should reflect the crime, not legislative interference. An eye for an eye, the old Hebrew dictum, is far superior to 99 years for victimless crimes and 2 years for murder. Those kinds of extremes lessen respect for the law. National laws that are fair and fast and proven to be impartial, work better than laws that comes out of political agendas.

How to reorganize the judicial system may take time to develop but if the same directives that alter bureaucracies apply to the legal system, it can happen. All agencies, bureaus and corporations that realize change, will promote the common good and the general welfare, a dream of our Founding Fathers. Our society will come to a point when our institutions won't work because they have been highjacked by a wealthy few who can't see the greater good. Change is needed.

GOD

Some have wondered how so short a name as God could stand for so large a concept. Different religions look at God with their own understandings. Eastern views want to include God in everything that is or could be. Western views want to separate God from everything that is. These two ways have both historic and cultural roots.

Judaism is the oldest Western religion. In its early period God was viewed as a tribal deity loyal to the Israelites but hardly able to cross Israel's borders. Other gods held sway in other lands. An early interpretation of the Commandment not to have any god before God was not to deny that other gods existed, but to enforce loyalty to the God of Israel. Later prophets would say that this God was the only real God; all others were false, weak influences conjured up by gentiles who did not know the only true God. Consequently, putting other gods before God meant putting anything in front of God to deny, compromise or otherwise trivialize one's respect, worship, loyalty and devotion to the One who is Eternal in fact and eternal in consciousness.

Christianity did not start with its concept of God where the Jews began but where they finally landed. God is eternal and superlative in all regards. All powerful, ever present, totally transcendent, yet totally immanent as well, God is likewise not the same as reality, the universe, creation, but other than creation. Thank Augustine for that view.

God became the stuff of theology: Christianity to be exact. Jewish theology is really more Jewish philosophy than theology though there were historic periods when Great Jewish thinkers living in Islamic held territories such as Moorish Spain, produced Jewish philosophy that resembled theology. The Moslems during their great empire period had rediscovered the Greek philosophers, particularly Plato and Aristotle. Aristotle's thought could be transposed into logical categories and logical categories applied to religious positions, leads to theology.

But Roman Catholicism has had a lock on theology since the Roman bishop regarded himself to be the successor of Peter. The Latin tongue would become the language of the church and the province of law, precisely because it leant itself to careful formulations from church approved statements. Since most church statements could be extrapolated from scripture, theology could demonstrate linkages to revelation.

All religions have scriptures. But not all religions regard their scriptures as pure revelation. Western religions have historically regarded their scriptures as directly inspired by God. Eastern scriptures regard their words inspired but through human agents, and thus the language of metaphor and imagery. Western religions from the period of Moses, understand some, most or all their words to be given directly from an eternal God speaking the tongue of the people receiving that word. Without the position of revelation, Western religions would become Western philosophies.

While many people have assumed God's reality, stating their assumption on the basis of faith or faith statements, many more have experienced something that they have identified as God present. Personal experience accounts for proof that God is real for those who attest that at some point and time they have been overwhelmed by a presence. Some have spoken of this presence as gentle, warm, loving and compassionate. For them it was not overwhelming but supportive. Was it God, or an angel, or an illusion brought on by stress, a chemical imbalance or an active imagination? How can anyone say with certainty? Our look at the phenomenal world involves our participation in this world. Since the introduction of Atomic Physics and Heisenberg's "Uncertainty Principle" nothing is certain since everyone effects what they encounter.

For this reason those religious expressions which do not identify a personal God cannot be discounted. In the case of Siddhartha Gautama's enlightenment no personal god was part of his experience. Siddhartha would thereafter be known as the Buddha, the Awakened One, not because he met God but because he was considered to be totally aware of the phenomenal world. For enlightened Buddhists, being aware of reality means seeing it as it is without preconceptions, definitions or selective perception. It means feeling, knowing, sensing and being conscious of a world in which you are a part, not a defined and separated participant. The Buddha's honesty is not in question. Buddhism insists on honesty as part of the Eightfold Path. The Buddha was indeed honest.

The Buddha discovered and taught that we make the world with our mind. As we think, so do we become. His reason for seeking the end of suffering was to change the experience of humans caught in an unsatisfactory earthly condition. Life is not satisfactory; life has suffering as part of its legacy. The Buddha did not seek union with God or the bliss associated with this union. He followed the strictest form of asceticism known to his day, subjugating his bodily needs to practically nothing; ignoring any and all of the pleasures that had characterized his life for the first twenty-nine years. Short of death, he suddenly realized that creating a condition of suffering would not solve the problem of suffering.

The ascetics he associated with were seeking union with what would always be beyond human limitation by creating severe human limitation. Siddhartha sought the end of suffering, not divine / human contact. In a flash of insight, he discovered the Middle Way, between extremes and opposites. It was not a matter of destroying his body that would answer his heartfelt quest, but maintaining a healthy body and clear mind, devoid of attachment to tastes, goals and anticipations. By uncovering the Four Noble Truths associated with humanity, he gave humanity a roadmap to follow out of the mire of repetitive unsatisfactory conditions.

The Buddha's way focused on this life in the now of existence. He was not primarily interested in a rewarded afterlife. He was interested in how to change now; a now that would transform a human's future nows.

Buddhism is considered atheistic. By definition, atheism is denying the reality of a personal God; a God who has personal characteristics. The Buddha, according to some Buddhist scriptures did not deny that gods exist, but that they do not warrant prayer, worship or even attention. He would say that they do not know the way to enlightenment. But acknowledging the temporary existence of multiply beings does not mean that what exists in a condition of eternal being does not exist. It is both a matter of experience and definition.

The Tao Te Ching, ostensibly written by Lao Tzu (the old Master) speaks of the Tao with no name who was before anything that came to be. The Tao is nothingness yet participates in everything that is. This view of what is eternal has dual qualities. It is primordial, before time and substance. It is also all substances, beings and matter. For Taoists, being in the flow of the Tao is to live ideally; to flow with events without judgment. It seems similar to the disciplined life of a Buddhist monk when he follows the Eightfold Path. Not passing judgment on one's moments, one lives in the immediate now of existence without projecting into possible future events or recalling past events. The mystically minded Taoist, like the almost enlightened Buddhist monk lives in the same present moment seeing reality as it is, without preconceptions, anticipation or judgments. But what if what the Buddhists call "What is" is the same as the "Tao", and is the same as what Western religions call the eternal God? What if the Tao is God by another name and Nirvana is God in verb expression?

The reality of what is and the reality of an eternal infinite God does not require proof. Certainly, God will always exist without someone attesting to that belief. Human experience presupposes that what we experience can somehow be subject to logical or phenomenological proof. It seems to be our nature to spin out proofs that only we can agree to. But if you start with the experience of others and then seek to duplicate that experience successfully, you don't have to prove it in words or profess it secondarily as accepted dogma. Its reality remains yours, and now becomes a part of who you are. Then your life becomes the proof and words only remind you of its reality.

The Taoists who actively live in the Tao and the Buddhists who actively live having blown out their skanda's energy, consciously know the reality of God. They know this because they are experiencing God in verb expression rather than in noun definition. Western religionists prefer nouns to verbs and therefore expanded definitions. But when Western religionists realize the noun of God as a verb, they enter into God's activity, ever changing, ever evolving, always doing.

For Eastern Religionists, be they Hindus, Buddhists or Taoists, reality is a verb. Define reality as God, as many Hindus do, and you begin to understand divine intelligence coupled with divine bliss. Those Buddhists who have had a flash of Nirvana or stepped into and stepped back into this world of consciousness, along with their Taoist cousins, all attest that it is superlatively wonderful, bliss filled and loving.

Nirvana is the sought for condition of Buddhists who hold the proposition that upon their physical death and having extinguished all attachments, the next natural step is to enter Nirvana. But the phrase "entering Nirvana" is a metaphor. No-one and nothing can enter Nirvana. Nirvana is a condition of nothingness, without things of any sort. It is a universal condition similar to the primordial Tao. So what enters Nirvana is nothing. The question then arises: why wish to be there? For the Buddhists, the answer is that once there, one need not return to this existence with its woes, wants and needs.

The 9th century Hindu yoga, Samkara, experienced the Godhead, the Totality, Brahman. Samkara is considered a monist, one who experienced God without qualities. Samkara would say, "All is God." There is nothing but God and what we see and experience as particular this and not that, is an illusion. He would say that God is not here or there, but everywhere. His verbal statements resemble the Tao and what Buddhists call "What Is." Was he less realistic than the Buddhist who preceded him? By announcing God to be all that is, he nevertheless indicated that those who believe in a personal deity do no harm themselves. The Vedanta teachers and Yogas who followed Samkara's monism would say that belief and worship of a personal God helps devotees to get in contact with God. Focusing on a person focuses on a personalized reality. That leads to having an object of devotion to relate to. These Yogas realized that we can draw near to a person rather than to Totality and thus enter into relationship.

Religious people, far more than mystical people, need relationship to sustain their religious fervor. Humans are more than intellectual beings. Humans are also feeling beings, sensing beings, recognizable interdependent beings. (Humans are interrelated beings but may choose not to recognize this intrinsic feature.) Taking Samkara's path is solitary, somewhat like becoming a Buddhist monk living in a sangha. The songha satisfies human community, but the prolonged periods in meditation can only be achieved by and in solitary silence.

The mystic quest for a direct experience with the invisible transcends his or her need for human companionship and support. It is the something more in their lives they lack and long for. It is one thing to profess belief in God or an intelligent infinite being; it is quite another to sense this to be true and long for the confirmation that closes the connection. There are different kinds of experience. One size does not fit all. The Bhakti Yoga devotee, as well as the Charismatic Christian, the Hasidic dancer, and the whirling Dervish may all experience what is greater than each is at other moments. Each may experience touching the infinite God without that experience being as conclusive as the mystic who feels enveloped, changed, and transformed.

The born again moment and the adult baptism event for Christians looking for a transforming moment may reflect an experience of being accepted, loved, and belonging. The ancient church didn't speak of becoming a christian as experiencing Christ but as joining the fellowship of believers.

As with other religions, joining through symbolic events isn't the same as experiencing God. It may point one in that direction but it doesn't substantiate a mountaintop encounter. Churches that require being born again do the same thing as churches that require confirmation. That moment, as witnessed by a community of like minded, authenticates a new beginning of belonging to that body. It does not authenticate an actual experience of transcendence. What churches who foster this requirement do is substitute membership for experience and an assured afterlife for this life enlightenment. For the seriously minded seeker neither confirmation nor being born again by committee is having a confirmed experience or being born to a new life. Both are poor substitutes for transcendence.

God remains a concept to be tested after death unless experienced in the now of life. The difference between "Now" in temporal time and "Now" in post life time is that "Now" lasts more than a millisecond. Authenticating God's reality in temporal time is to know God for all time and beyond time. It is to know both the experience of eternal change and changelessness. Both change and changelessness characterize what is eternal and what is God. Change is how God acts as a verb in creation. Changelessness is how God essentially is in nothingness. Nothingness is both God's domain and God, infinite and beyond definition; defined by His ethical intention and beyond the limits of ethical boundaries. Infinite love comes close to recognizing God's nature and intention. Infinite righteousness comes close to encountering God's appearance.

Polytheism, the belief in many gods, has an interesting history. In the West, the belief in many gods resembles an extended family unit, sometimes even a Fraternity House. One god assumes the role of head of the extended family. Others in the unit distinguish themselves by the gifts they bring or the chosen roles they play. Often the role of a god reflects a natural event. Thunder, sunshine, the moon, the wind all example different functions associated with different gods who are part of a family overlooking a culture or nation.

The Nordic tribes had specific gods and goddesses known for their function, interest and character. Ancient civilizations, Greece and Mesopotamia for example, had a pantheon of men and women who watched over the empire blessing it when they offered appropriate sacrifices and leaving it when they were displeased. The notion of primary causation comes from the belief that natural catastrophic events are caused for any number of reasons by godlike beings directly. Homer and the Iliad speak of the Greek gods directly interfering in the affairs of specific men who displeased them while other gods felt compelled to come to their rescue.

The Indian gods likely came out of the belief system of the Aryans who invaded the Indus Valley. Some may have come from the Dasas or Drividian people subjugated by the Aryans. These gods acted on the spells of the Brahmin priests who knew the exact Sanskrit words to chant to bring an appropriate blessing. With the appearance of Buddhism in India, the power of the gods shifts and the power of the priests diminishes.

In China, the cosmology reflects a more egalitarian landscape. Ancients believed that the gods were all once men and women. The first man to die evolved in the heavens (Tien) until he became the old man of the sky, Shang Ti. His role as head of the gods is questionable; his position as first among equals is not. As people died and did not return in other bodies to earth, the proportion of interested entities grew to gigantic numbers. All or most of a person's descendants were in Tien watching the affairs of their descendants. Not all would become gods. Those who suffered and sacrificed innocently likely became gods. Those who made significant contributions became gods. Kung Fu Tzu, or Confucius, was proclaimed a god by emperor Wo Ti during the Han dynasty in the early CE period. It could be assumed that so great a moral and intellectual figure deserved this honor. The fact that the Han emperors saw Confucius' teaching as a stabilizing influence didn't hurt. Confucius' directives officially became accepted.

Two things are especially significant about Tien or heaven. First, an early belief that duality defines reality. Thus Yin and Yang, dual opposites arising from the One, grew to find definition in all of reality and life. Yin was the moon, passive, reflecting, silent. Yang was the sun, aggressive, bright, initiating and sometimes life destroying. The earth was held to be extreme Yin while the sky or Tien was seen as extreme Yang. Thus, those residing in Tien would be on the active side as they witnessed the affairs of men and especially men who held power and control.

Second, at the time of the Chou Dynasty, a new belief grew to dominate Chinese thought. The Mandate of Heaven, as it was to be called, may have come in with the Chou's or it may predate the Chou dynasty. At the time of Kung Fu Tzu, The Mandate of Heaven, becomes a moral force, as well as a way to authenticate the position of emperor. Kung Fu Tzu was a moral thinker. Favoring the common people, he felt their pain. Trying to change the power driven attitude of those in power, he saw Tien as both above and governing the affairs of men.

The Mandate of Heaven simply states that it is heaven who awards a Mandate to the emperor to govern. Like the Western notion that kings are God's anointed or that kings have a divine right to rule, the Chinese Mandate of Heaven says an emperor holds his position with heaven's approval. When the approval changes and the Mandate shifts to another candidate, things happen. Hurricanes, floods, earthquakes, tornadoes, droughts, plagues all can occur until the emperor and his company are gone from the scene and a new administration is installed. If the new emperor is benevolent, fair, just and inclined to help the populace, catastrophic events subside and Tien, or heaven is pleased to bless the earth.

Natural explanations can easily replace primary causation in explaining catastrophic events. What the Mandate of Heaven explains is that what happens on earth is interrelated with what happens above the earth. It is both an environmental and social judgment on human designs of power and greed interfering with natural balance, harmony and distribution.

God as the product of defined revelation simplifies what we may think of God. God as natural subject leads to a pluralistic understanding that considers Eastern cosmologies as having a developmental reality. Western Religious notions must define and therefore limit understanding the primal reality of God infused in what is. Revelation needs to take stories, metaphors and language and simplify them to actual events, literal realities and empirical facts. But the nature of reality and our ability to perceive anything is rapped up in symbols, physiological limitations and selective perception. Our ability to see and understand anything directly is nearly impossible, given the way our consciousness works. The eye can only see straight and wavy lines. The brain, governed by selective memory, accepted learned perceptions and fight/flight dispositions, can only accept what it is prepared to see and understand. Like the proverbial goldfish released into the ocean, unprepared to recognize its new environment, we are drawn to what is familiar, safe and clearly defined.

Simple logic, when coupled with metaphysics, naturally moves to understanding God succinctly as Tao, functionally as Sat/Chit/Ananda and relationally as Yin/Yang parent. What develops from these simple functional understandings may not help our personal psychology but they move us to realize that God as reality does not need believers. Drawing to the One who is center of all that is or could be, by identifying God as Father/Mother/friend/righteous perfection, also aides us to see ourselves as inheritors, divine children and worthy partners.

What the mystics experienced as oneness with the Divine is the natural state, less what we have created by our ego consciousness. Human evolution required separation, and ego consciousness is the mechanism that maintains separation. It is not about megalomania, or neurotic/psychotic hallucinations. It is about seeing for the first time without our earthly parent's eyes or society's norms or culturally defined and historically learned standards. The Omega Man of Pierre Teilhard de Chardin appears to be there. The realized Arhat appears to be there. The enlightened Yoga master seems to have lifted the veil. The Jewish Kabbalist has entered the holy. God is natural and our return to be part of God is natural. What is unnatural is our sense of ourselves and the perceived identity of others. What is unnatural is any reason to kill, destroy or hurt another.

If Samkara was totally correct, along with his Buddhist brothers, then hurting another is hurting oneself. While the Godhead does not suffer, the god within draws further within. The history of the world reflects shrunken gods within caught in their own fears, harmful actions and evil designs, suffering future experiences to break a cycle of their own making. The god within does not suffer anymore than the Totality. But the god within sees and experiences everything as if from afar, including the activities, feeling states and situational moments of its physical/psychological host. The more it experiences, the more it must return to a physical condition to undo its mistakes. God allows freedom so we can make mistakes. God is freedom so we can learn who we are in relationship.

For the East, the emphasis is on infinity, nothingness and tranquility. For the West, the emphasis is on identity, particularity and definition. The West prizes relationship. It prizes relationship with God, the world and human beings. The West perceives relationship as nouns participating with nouns; persons participating with persons. Relationship can only be perceived as one particular to another. We can't relate to infinity as a particular this and not that. Persons relate to persons. Beings relate to beings.

Much has been written about our relationship with God via the Christian model. When the church proclaimed Jesus as God at the Council of Nicea in 325 CE and then went on to establish the Trinity as doctrine, it affirmed the Apostolic Party of Bishops as the only authentic type of Christianity permitted. Jesus was a man, a person, a particular different from the God of the Jews as understood and worshipped.

The notion of Heavenly Father was not new. The Jews of Jesus' day regarded God as Heavenly Father. That made God a person, with relational qualities. As Christianity developed through the persecution period sponsored by imperial Rome, how the Jews experienced God stayed in place for the budding Christians. What they added, was his Son as intrinsically connected to God as his only Son. But Jesus had never announced he was God's only Son. In fact, Jesus enjoined those who heard him to regard God as their Heavenly Father as well. That movement away from what Jesus had said, made Jesus a God who could compete with the Pagan gods.

The first Christian Church was composed of Jews who believed Jesus to be the Messiah, the anointed of God. This was a Jewish notion. Those Jews held Jesus as such because they had witnessed his resurrection and believed that event confirmed his authority. God had raised him out of death and would therefore restore the kingdom of God to Israel. A group of converts came from the Greek educated faction. This group practiced the less severe requirements of the Torah. Gentiles converted to Christianity from this group because they were drawn to Judaism for its ethical teachings. A faction of gentiles had attended Synagogue services throughout the Roman Empire. The beauty, directness and righteousness of the Jewish religion made more sense than the pantheon of self absorbed gods of Greek and Roman traditions coupled with the development of emperor worship. Their sincerity drew them to what they must have sensed as true.

By the second century, Rome's posturing had effectively reduced this faction to a small number. The Apostolic Party continued to bravely endure Roman persecution. They held to the position that they had received the true message from the apostles who had gotten it from Jesus himself. The succession of information would become a succession of authoritative positions identified as the Office of Bishop. Other Christian groups quietly maintained a different tradition. This faction would be known by the blanket term, Gnostic. The Gnostics flew under Imperial Rome's radar because they observed Roman polity and practice. Later they would be condemned.

The first three centuries became a formative period for the Christian Church. While under Roman persecution many expressions of Christianity existed side by side. While those called Gnostics held different beliefs, some felt that Jesus the man did not actually die. A dead savior was not worth worshipping. But they did gravitate to what they viewed as secret teachings given by Jesus to those able to understand them. Some, like the Jewish Ebonites, believed in the physical resurrection but also held to a Jewish Messiah who would always be subservient to God the Father. They would refuse to be Trinitarians while still observing the Torah. After Constantine, the Gnostics would be banned from the Empire. If they did not convert to the position of the official party approved by the emperor they would either need to leave Roman held territory or be condemned to death. Ebonites chose to flee still maintaining their beliefs into the sixth century CE.

How did these changes effect belief in God. For the Jews and early Jewish Christians, God was almighty, alone in power and identity. Jesus was either a well intentioned prophet or the Messiah who would return to establish his kingdom. By the Third and finally Fourth century, gentile Christians saw him as more than a prophet. He was alive and getting ready to return in triumph. This moreness would find expression in defining him as God, not in the role of Father, but in the role of Son. The Holy Spirit was thrown in for good measure. After all, God's Spirit appeared throughout the Christian Old Testament. Without the Holy Spirit there would be divine duality.

Thus God, once alone and superlative in all categories, would discover Himself part of an exclusive family founded on function and revelation. Providing this as an applied doctrine became the province of a latin educated, Greek supported, electorate of approved Church fathers and dignitaries. Roman legal language would wed Greek philosophical categories to form a tradition that is still in place. How much is inspired by God's Spirit and how much is the work of dedicated church theologians is a mute point after two thousand years.

If we were to go back to the BCE period, prior to the influence of Roman jurisprudence, Greek schools and codified Jewish Law, we might see God differently. The model being proposed and representing a conclusion coming out of previous comments and concepts, is to understand God as infinite, ever-present activity. Rather than a noun, defined by other nouns, God is able to both communicate and incarnate at will. This conclusion holds God as other and immanent. As other, God is beyond definition but not intention. As immanent, God's Spirit is present in all people from Adam through Jesus. But certain people play a truly significant role in helping others discover God as other but involved. Abraham discovers his purpose and identity as the father of a nation. Moses discovers God's voice and will, and being able to write, transcribes that divine will for God's people to follow. Jesus discovers that he is directly related to this voice and will. He is son and heir to God's plan for all people. By remaining true to his father's will and voice, he gives humanity a new identity that is both noun and verb.

How does this new identity appear? For one thing, it acknowledges Jesus as the first fruits of god/men and women. As Jesus realized his relationship, so he invites others to do the same. Not as only Son, but as unique son of many other sons and daughters, Jesus acts as divine symbol, mold and function of what children of God are to look like. Calling him Lord is not diminished. Calling him brother is included. The more we relate to him the more we see the face of God in human form, compassionate, loving, forgiving, righteous, truthful and beyond self absorbed ego. His identity becomes our identity. His discovery becomes our discovery. The Trinity becomes a symbolic representation of how God operates: as provider, partner, friend, lover, and uniter.

Nor does this understanding diminish all the saints who have honored both Jesus and the Trinity. It includes all people who faithful to God's intentional rules of conduct, realize they are directly related to that infinite source who enfolds all life. The writer of Revelation envisioned a new heaven and a new earth, one in which lion and lamb lie down together in peace. It appears on this earth after all violence, greed, fear and dishonesty are spent. The realized Kingdom of God Jesus taught is an extended community of like minded, totally integrated, lovingly bonded, who have finally arrived within themselves to acknowledge others as equal in potential and actuality. God in each becomes God in all. The life force in each produces evolved persons faithful to creation and connected to the creator who sees that it is good.

Theology divides because it must. Spirituality becomes the norm of behavior and presence. Theology is relegated to ways men devise to call attention to themselves. Spirituality becomes the language of the soul who knows his and her father. Jesus stands alongside this happy company, forever respected and loved for bringing so great a company back to God.

The many religions that have frequented this earth over eons of time will come together in recognition of their true brotherhood, united in identity and intention. This model envisions all who call on God as Father and do His will, to be not only included in this vast array of mortals, evolved and realized, but also honored for their role in seeing and hearing God. The mystics who see God will stand alongside those who have heard God speak through His law and acted accordingly. The pious who have done all in their power to help others will recognize the ones they have helped as God in disguise. This conclusion will not please everyone, for it presupposes that God has set in motion mechanisms to afford souls multiple life experiences to bring them to the point of redemption. For the Christian faction, redemption starts with recognizing Jesus' deeds, death and words. It doesn't end there. It ends when those who have started here arrive at self identification of who they are and who they really belong to. For those who have chosen divine nothingness as their final arrival, God as infinite nothingness, has already rewarded them by divine inclusion in all that is. For those in the West, paradise, heaven and the kingdom will be divine community in realized time and space.

ETHICS

Ethics is the compilation of acts involving others. Morality is closely related to Ethics but can be defined as doing what is moral, having a moral disposition and being moral. Morality includes how you think of yourself and how you treat yourself. Ethics involves how you treat others and what you believe to be the ethical conduct you would engage in to augment your relationship with others. Ethical conduct cannot be done by itself, it must include others. But ethical conduct also includes your intentions as well as your actions. It may be assumed that intention toward the other one will carryover into your actions, which in turn will create an effect. Thus, ethical thinking and conduct have a moral effect germinating from a related cause.

Hindus have a term, "Karma" that refers to the moral law pervading the universe and all reality. Karma is the Law of Cause and Effect, or Cause and Consequence. Karma has its physical counterpart in the Principle of Causation. Science has based its total line of experimentation and discovery on causation. Putting ingredients together, supplying energy in most cases, and awaiting results is not conducted in total ignorance. The experimentator has an expectation as to what will happen based on what was done. For Eastern religionists that translates into Karma or the moral equivalent of Physical Causation. For Buddhists, Karma is the result of the total interrelatedness of everything and everyone. For Hindus, Karma is the Law set in motion to guide people back to God.

Ethical conduct has an effect. Karma has a consequence. Ethical conduct either depreciates another or enhances the other. All of the major religions in the world today have ethical teachings central to their practice. From time to time certain of these teachings rise to a level of disproportionate importance. That was the situation when Father Augustine promoted divine grace above the divinely instituted human responsibility to behave in an ethical manner. Augustine did not do that to negate ethics but to affirm his belief that human activity can not stand up to what God does on Man's behalf. He considered that ethical conduct should be one's response to divine intervention, not a competing factor for salvation.

Martin Luther would defy the Roman Catholic Church, based on Augustine's central discovery, by promoting the gift of Faith above any good works or ethical conduct a person would engage in. Thus, Faith, became the central teaching informing all other religious beliefs. Over time, Faith would be subsumed under a momentary experience of "being born again." Luther's chief argument with the religious institution of his day was their authoritarian posture that relegated the bible to fragmented actions sponsored by specific Church dignitaries, principally the Pope. Church tradition could contradict both scripture and conscience because it had the authority to do so. Luther said no to that principle and would successfully break away from the consequence of his own painful death by forming an alliance with the power structure of his day. Without their support all would have failed.

For Western religious consciousness, ethics began when Moses encountered God and brought down the Law from Mount Sinai. The Law he gave the people could be summarized in the Ten Commandments. Jews also hold an Oral tradition Moses gave his people. The Mishnah, as it was known, would expand to the First century CE. Roman slaughter of Jews would lead distinguished Rabbis to begin to write down the Mishnah, adding commentary until it was completed by the Sixth Century CE to become the Talmud. The Tanakh or Christian Old Testament and the Talmud would then comprise the total ethical teachings Jews follow to current times.

Western Christian consciousness would add the New Testament accounts of Jesus, Paul, John, Peter, James and the unknown writer of Hebrews to fill out Christian ethical teachings for centuries to come. When the Apostolic Party arose to prominence with the final victory of Constantine, that understanding of Christianity became the sole form acceptable to the now Byzantium Empire. The Byzantine Empire was the Old Roman Empire transplanted to Constantinople, Turkey without the accepted polytheism of the old order. Rome became the seat of power for the Roman bishop now isolated from the main army of the Empire. It wasn't long before Germanic tribes tested the hated Roman Empire's defenses in Italy. A series of invasions, starting with the Visigoth army of Alaric conquered the eternal city. What followed were a number of invasions, until the various tribal systems had migrated through Italy to finally land on land they chose to settle.

Eastern religious consciousness evolved differently and thus the ethical teachings found in these religions make a slightly different appearance. Confucius was a moral teacher. So his teachings carry a moral tone of "ought" that spells out how to achieve peace and social harmony. The Buddha taught precepts to those who would listen, that moved people away from a perpetual condition of suffering to a final condition of bliss. Unknown and known Hindu teachers announced truths that would finally eliminate negative karma in order to secure an eternal state of liberated union with the Divine. Confucius was never interested in union with God, but in creating a state of social order that would respect all players. The Buddha saw reality as it is and sought to convey a regiment of living that would open human eyes to see themselves as an integral part of the natural order.

While Eastern sages and enlightened masters taught different specifics they all agreed on basic ethical truths. Ethics heals the human condition. Ethics brings deep satisfaction to those committed to living that way. Ethics unites humanity and all life forms by suppressing ego selfishness that tends toward harm, hate and oppression. Ethics reaches out, respects differences and unites commonalities. At the heart of ethics is the understanding that all people, whatever their color, race, ethnic identity or gender, are equally important. Most ethical teachings presuppose a divine judge whose original intentions become ethical understandings. Living ethically, intentionally and actively, connects to divine intention at all levels.

Those Eastern religious expressions that do not promote a personal supreme God nevertheless support a supreme purpose and process, they view as totally natural. Call it by any name you wish, the result is the same and therefore the effects are the same. Humanists who don't wish to become affiliated with any religion, practice ethical principles in keeping with religious people who worship their own understanding of God. That is not by accident. There is something innately present in normally developed human beings that instinctively knows right from wrong behavior and thus is able to recognize ethical conduct.

A significant faction of Western religionists and all but a few Eastern religionists, agree that when people do what is right, ethical and just, their reward or effect is the same as the result or effect of those who practice the teachings of their religion, whatever it is. This understanding is both promoted by the various scriptures and good sense. If a personal God oversees the universe or if the universe simply is what it is, woven together by interrelated events, doing what is right and just, and living in an ethical fashion according to standards of conduct that enrich humanity and promote social harmony, create a positive result that carries over past this life in keeping with its developed energy. Add to that a definition of human identity that includes a permanent or semi permanent condition of being or soul, and you have a good reason to live within divine intention. Subscribing to divine intention insures a pleasant afterlife free of facing self induced unethical actions.

What are ethical actions that comprise ethical conduct? Generally, they include actions that enhance other people, displaying respect for their physical body, aspirations and well-being. Ethical conduct can include all of nature, once one is clear that human beings are part of nature. Unethical conduct may include indirect actions that create deleterious effects over time. Non-immediate negative consequences may be legal and thus immune from prosecution, but they are not ethical when people are made to suffer loss or pain or health because of a product or process whose immediate effect avoids those consequences, but whose long range effect produces various injurious results.

Specifically, ethical principles involve a quality of relationship. How do we interact with others? What are our intentions? If we interact in a positive way that permits mutual respect, the likelihood is we are acting ethically. If our intentions are to help others, the likelihood we are ethically intentioned. To insure that we are not deceiving ourselves, Moses has given us clear guidelines we call the Ten Commandments. Jesus spelled out which intentions would best insure we were acting from the most appropriate motivation. He placed loving God over everything else as first, and loving neighbor as ourselves as second. Both rules are quotes from his Tanakh. For Western religionists, be you Jew, Christian or Moslem, the combination of these commandments insures your ethical behavior. For the Western secularists, practicing mutual respect, along with respect for all life forms will do.

Perhaps it would be constructive to move away from generalities to specifics and point out why these specifics demonstrate ethical conduct. The Ten Commandments, a summary of the other mitzvahs found in the Tanakh, may be specific enough. To be ethical is to provide an environment of truthful communication, non-oppressive behavior, nonintrusive interactions, respect for another's relationships, property and livelihood, and avoiding hurting or killings others.

Let's see if these rules match up with the prohibitions mentioned in Deuteronomy 5?
1) Worship only the one real God, not things or conditions.
2) Make no idols that come out of yourself
3) Don't ask the Infinite for selfish things
4) Respect those who nurture you and provide for you.
5) Don't take life
6) Don't break up family units or marriage relationships
7) Don't take what is not yours
8) Don't desire what is not yours and belongs to another
What makes these ethical? For one thing, they suppress ego wants, moving the person to selfless behavior. For another thing, they encourage mutual social behavior that demonstrates respect for others and the property of others. They show how not to hurt or injure another by what one does and does not do. They also show that the one practicing these mitzvahs is psychologically balanced enough not to exhibit obsessive wants and behavior that infringe on the rights of others and ultimately hurt or knowingly destroy them.

When we look at ethical teachings arising in Eastern religions we encounter much the same qualities. Confucius' ethics come out of rules for creating social harmony and peaceful living. Mutual respect is high on the Eastern list of attitudes to have and demonstrate. Interior evolution is also high on the Eastern list. One evolves to a superior, spiritual state where ego needs are minimized and interrelated recognitions maximized. Confucius' superior man is a person of honor, integrity, honesty, generosity, responsibility and humility. For the Buddha, getting out of this woe of suffering means not becoming attached to ego needs that take rather than give; want rather than leave; long for rather than appreciate. Buddhist ethics allows no room for greed, self aggrandizement or dishonest discourse.

Hindu ethics may not reach far enough to help those in desperate need, considering their condition to be a result of their own karmic decisions. But Hindu ethics is also aware that not doing good works prolongs one's eternal return to this life. So, to unite with Brahman, or God, the devotee is encouraged to exhibit positive emotions and helpful actions, releasing all credit to the god within. Competition for life itself hinders selfless actions, yet selfless acts move one closer to recognizing the eternal God who is all there is or could be. Selfish acts close off this recognition, focusing on what is not eternal or ultimately real. The various Yoga schools have different foci but the same intention; that is, to move from small self to large Self. To do this one must live by ethical principles.

Two legs describe the religious person. The religious person stands on the leg of experience and the leg of ethical actions. Experience of God offers both confirmation of God's reality, and the happiness of being connected to all that is. Ethical living offers the experience of doing God's intentions, free of self limiting intentions fostered by selfish ego states of mind. Ethical living connects the religious person with life, God and creation. Doing that which connects one, creates the joy of belonging. Humanity is not to be castigated but honored. The spark of divinity and eternality is freed from one's myopic perception without divine intention, to a universal perception that sees reality as it is eternally and in the mind of God. With these two legs the religious person can run, jump, sit, stand and move in God's direction. Without these two legs, he or she is frozen to self.

The reason both East and West hold to the same ethical teachings is because these ethical teachings have been given to humanity. What is eternal has intention. To move to the source of that intention one must exercise that intention while experiencing that Presence. Western mystics discover the Presence of God and are changed. Practicing ethical principles moves in the same path God moves and thus walks in God's footprints and along God's path. Ethical people who seriously practice ethics live moral lives rich with the presence of the One they may or may not recognize, but who will recognize them with eternality. Mystics practice ethical rules of conduct because they know that the Divine practices them as well.

Can we specifically identify ethical principles without limiting them to a specific number? That is what summarizing them does. But they form around specific attitudes and actions nicely. Having a generous nature leads to a generous display toward those not as well off who also need and would accept help from a nonjudgmental benefactor. **Generosity** *is more than giving money or goods; it is demonstrating a spirit of sharing cognizant that while some have much more than others, all are intrinsically equal in worth and personal identity.*

__Honesty__ refers to being straight in what information you disclose, share and wish to communicate. Its value is that it instills trust and thus connects you to the one hearing or seeing the information you share. At some unconscious level people can sense when someone is lying or concealing the truth. Honest statements confirm what others already sense and thus build connections. When people are afraid of some danger, they may accept dishonest explanations spoken to assuage their fears, but once the fear is placated, the realization that they were lied to comes to the fore. If the lying continues, the people lied to will finally label the liar for who he is and for what he did. Truth does come out, even in the midst of rationalizations and further coverups. It is the nature of honesty to claim the field after the combatants have been driven away. Honesty is precisely an ethical value because God is totally honest, once we can recognize him. What makes Jesus a clear reflection of the eternal God is precisely that he was totally honest. Being totally honest is being totally transparent.

***Mutual Respect** is an ethical principle because it acknowledges others as equals and treats them as such. People sense if you respect them for who they are and what they are. It doesn't mean automatically accepting what they say or do. It means hearing what they say and respecting what they do. Even in War, combatants can respect each other across the battlefield because each has done his best to win while honoring the prisoner of war status of captured or fallen combatants. In this case, when enemies fight by a code of honor, mutual respect is appropriate. When one side plays by no rules, it is not. Even in war, there is a code of honor that warrants a begrudging mutual respect.*

*Honor often refers to how one conducts himself or herself. Honor implies personal dignity. **Dignity** is witnessed by anyone encountering the person possessing it. It can be mistaken for arrogance, but it has a different quality. A person with dignity honors the other while not expecting the other to honor him. In the face of loss, pain, failure or death, the one possessing honor doesn't lash out, decrying his lot, but accepts it with dignity and bears witness to everyone present how high human identity can rise in the face of overwhelming odds. Honor does not cower or grovel. Honor meets its physical end knowing itself as genuine, and that it will be rewarded accordingly. That which is eternal is there to greet the one who exhibits honor and leaves this world with dignity. Life's reversals cannot destroy or even conquer honor and dignity, two of the many signs of continuous life and purpose.*

Justice is an ethical principle emphasized by Western religions. In Judaism, Justice forms one of the trinitarian principles close to what distinguishes Judaism. **Justice, Righteousness** *and* **Mercy** *are each held as what Gods does and Man is called to do. Justice means being just and fair. God is just and fair and thus people called to belong to God are to be just and fair in their dealings with any and all others, Jews and Gentiles alike. Righteousness fits with Justice because doing what is right before God is doing what is just for all concerned. To do justice is to act righteously, to act in a right manner and thus honor God who acts in a right manner with all people. Mercy describes God because God is merciful and compassionate. But God's compassion is God's plea to humankind to honor his commandments and his intentions. Thus, Justice, Mercy and Righteousness obey God's wishes and promote human relationships (Micah 6:8).*

Justice is attached to the Judgment day, a terrible day of the Lord when God will settle accounts with humankind. For Jews and Moslems, the Judgment Day is the moment Justice is done universally. Those who have not practiced Righteousness, Justice and Mercy will feel their misdeeds themselves. Jesus said as much when he told the parable of the unforgiving servant who chose not to forgive a minor debt of a fellow servant after he himself had been forgiven a major debt by the master. All those who do not forgive or show mercy, will not be shown mercy by God. Islam and Judaism both concur. For them the Judgment Day is the Day of ultimate Justice.

Christianity had a similar belief for what constitutes the Judgment Day, but somehow lost sight of this central understanding. Those Christians who look forward to Jesus' Second Coming see the final Judgment as one in which all those professing Jesus as God's elect, are saved while all others are condemned to damnation. That view crept into the Church with Christianity's formal acceptance as the only approved religion. References in the Book of Revelation and Paul's letters have been interpreted to mean belief in Jesus Christ preempts Justice, Righteousness and Mercy expressed on the human level. Such a deviation has created a false trust in faith, grace and being born again, above the transformation that occurs when people practice God's ethical demands. It is that ethical transformation, beyond theological positioning and proclamational assurances, that affords humans with the proper wedding garment to meet God. If belief in Jesus, along with following him by emulating what he did, is practiced than his followers can be assured of a happy homecoming. Belief goes with practice, and practice is practicing the ethical teachings Jesus practiced himself.

In Islam, the final Judgment is described in graphic terms meant to compel submitters to obey God's teachings without reservation. The Day of Judgment is too late for those who have put off practicing God's intentions because time will stand still and freedom of action become the final consequence for what was not done by those who chose not to act in a righteous manner and with a just and compassionate heart.

***Gratitude** is an ethical principle. Gratitude acknowledges that we are all interconnected and interrelated. Being connected means we are not alone metaphysically or circumstantially. We become grateful when we realize that our lives are filled with divine and human purpose. The divine side sees a just and merciful God who supplies all our needs. The human side develops an attitude of gratitude able to meet adversities with positive, helpful feelings. In effect, a grateful attitude invites the universe to help us in whatever ways it chooses. Gratitude leads to **Happiness,** another ethical principle confident in a good outcome. You can't defeat a happy person, grateful for his state of mind and circumstance. You can only defeat him if he gives up by surrendering his happiness and gratitude.*

*Happiness leads to **Joy,** a spiritual ethical principle. Joy heals the body and mind and looks forward to encountering the author of all joy who saw that it was good. Joy then automatically becomes bliss the final state of being, reserved for those who see God and willingly disappear into his universal being. That is how the Hindus describe Brahman. Brahman is Total Being, Total Consciousness and Total Bliss. It doesn't get any better than that. An ungrateful attitude closes off blessings and thus justifies unhappiness. Unhappiness can't claim any joy and thus can't realize any bliss. The ego has shut down all systems that could improve the person's condition. Misery and death must follow, either at one's own hand or one's own degenerating body functions.*

__Peace__ is a powerful ethical principle. Confucius developed his philosophy to create the environment for peace. Peace leads to __Harmony__, another ethical principle. When peace exists, harmony has an opportunity to work. Harmony and Peace together illicit __Cooperation,__ another ethical principle often overlooked. Cooperation is far better than competition. Cooperation feeds harmony and peaceful interactions. For Christians, one need only go to the Sermon on the Mount in the Gospel of Matthew to recognize how important peace was to Jesus. "Blessed are the peacemakers for they shall be called the sons (and daughters) of God."

In Jesus' day many Jews understood themselves as sons of God. While the church would later claim that Peter's confession of faith, announcing that Jesus was the Christ, the son of the living God, would make Jesus assume a unique role in the Godhead, that understanding at the time of Peter would not have existed. For Peter, Jesus was the Messiah and also a fellow son of the living God. But Jesus did tie sonship to peacemaking, not conflict production. Ultimately, those who see God as related, have an attitude of peace, There is no discord in God's presence. Therefore, only those with peace in their consciousness and harmony in their being and an attitude of cooperation in their social awareness have a place at the table of God. They can claim sonship and daughtership because they enjoy being together and enjoy being with what is eternally real and true, almighty God. All ethical teachings and principles are peace producing. They all fit together.

__Love__ is an ethical principle. It is the basis of creation. Love binds beings together. It describes God as personal, for what is personal is capable of love. More than a force, God is a loving source who creates out of love, much as a mother bears a child out of love. Creation has been described by Christian mystics as God birthing creation, life, things in distinction to nothing. As an important ethical principle it motivates the other ethical principles, allowing each space yet informing each of the other, and the central source who and what gives meaning to what is and could become.

Last, but not least in our description of ethical principles is __Prophesy__. Prophesy does not exhaust specific ethical principles, but the others not mentioned here derive from the ones already mentioned. The Christian New Testament speaks of prophesy as preaching and uses a Greek word which means preaching. The Tanakh speaks of it in Hebrew as speaking for God directly. In fact, the understanding of Revelation in distinction to Inspiration, came from the Hebrew prophets who would begin their announcement with: "Thus says the Lord." Prophesy is the __Prophetic Voice__, an ethical principle not appreciated by those whose unethical actions and intentions have long silenced the prophets of old. The Prophetic Voice speaks truthfully of what it knows on behalf of God whose intentions have been compromised by dishonest, selfish and power driven mortals. Its message is simple: "Get back to the intentions of God as spoken, and then written in His Commandments." Do those and you shall live.

In the remaining pages the opposite of ethical principles will be spelled out. Opposite means in opposition to Divine intention. That which is intrinsically unethical pervades our economic and political system significantly. Socialistic governmental systems exhibit a measure of unethical actions. Perhaps, because they represent older cultures who have had enough of war and devastation, they have learned to control their unethical tendencies. Perhaps, they have evolved past their myopic dictatorial philosophies to embrace more humanitarian views of maintaining society. Whatever the case, they more closely resemble a more ethical system than the one promoted as Capitalistic. Capitalism is not the same as democracy. Capitalism is the economic policy that drives what we call our democracy. It is not the same because Capitalism operates as an oligarchy, representing and governed by the wealthy and powerful at the expense of the rest of society.

Money is not in itself unethical. It is simply the medium of exchange. In a commercially driven system, goods and services are exchanged for the medium of exchange. People work for, invest for and create for money. All of that is not unethical. It becomes unethical when unethical principles influence it to the point of controlling it. In a capitalistic system one does not make enough money. There is never enough because money loses it's value when it stops flowing. Jesus said that the love of money is the root of all evil. The Tanakh says much the same thing. The love of money is greed and greed is the unethical principle driving our economy.

Greed, Dishonesty and Power are the trinitarian unethical principles that, over time, characterize a capitalistic system in distinction to Justice, Mercy and Righteousness that characterize religious ethical principles. In a competitive social system where wealth dominates, greed encourages dishonesty, which in turn encourages power. Political Parties strive for power and control. That is the true nature of politics, not negotiation and compromise. Power drives toward an absolute condition while dishonesty is viewed as necessary to create optimal results. Dishonesty becomes the currency of Parties and corporations seeking control over an uninformed populace. Money allows uneven influence in the political process.

Money drive the Media, once viewed as a servant of the people acting in their best interests, to spread sensationalism in place of information. Information is skewed to favor the powerful, silencing or ignoring deviant voices crying for equity. The old dictatorships of totalitarian governments have been replaced by communication machines that favor commercial sources. Money drives everything: the media who need money to compete, increase and control the airways; the commercial systems that bombard all media with incessant advertisements; the political campaigns that need to get elected; industries that produce inferior goods and services: large corporations that increase profits at the expense of salaries and living standards. Money in the hands of fewer and fewer players, moves toward a two class social system of rich and poor and a small select middle class of ambitious want-a-be's.

The footprints of Greed, Dishonesty and Power are everywhere. The common denominator is money and its acquisition. Greed does not know when to stop because it is intrinsically obsessive. Dishonesty doesn't know when to stop because it appears beyond accountability. Power doesn't know when to stop because it has lost its ability to serve the greater good. Both major political parties need money and power. One believes the common man is unable to govern himself, and thus favors a few knowing what is best for the many. The other favors the working class, but hasn't learned to communicate ethical principles that resonate with the people. One speaks often about religion without being ethical. The other doesn't speak about religion and thus appears unethical. Unlike the European parliamentary system which can oust a government when it looses favor with the people, our system must wait for scheduled voting periods, allowing a badly motivated administration time to discredit or even eliminate political opposition with dishonest campaigns.

All of these unethical principles are in opposition to God's ethical ideals set in motion to bring people together for benevolent results. Oppression is an unethical principle showing itself today in economic deprivation. As the rich get to be super rich and the middle class become the poor class, power shifts from the many to the few. That is by design and the natural consequence of an unethical economic and political system challenging minor players to alter its momentum. The future appears bleak unless enough people take ethics seriously.

Our forefathers brought on this continent a new nation conceived in life, liberty and the pursuit of happiness. Life is ultimately only available when ethical principles are in place and practiced. Liberty is not doing what you want or earning as much as you can get away with. It is allowing each to be free enough to benefit oneself and others without hurting any. The pursuit of happiness is not a material fortress unassailable by any but the more powerful. It is a spiritual state of mutual respect that connects people to one another. Our Founding Fathers knew the face of oppression. That is why they came here. They created a government of checks and balances, not one of political will, that envisioned people being safe from unethical persons bent on power and control.

*Ethics works best when it is universally practiced. When it is verbalized but not practiced, nature assumes the prophetic voice. When greed is rationalized as necessary to help a free economy, no one ultimately benefits. Confucius hated greed. He believed in and warned of the Mandate of Heaven. Heaven ultimately judges the earth. Weather changes create enough suffering and devastation until the government that caused natural forces to revolt, are silenced. Because ethical principles are divinely instituted they are also naturally expressed. When they are frustrated from doing what they were meant to do, the prophetic voice takes the shape of nature in conflict with earth. The choice is with those who change the direction they are heading. There is always time for a change in direction by recognizing real ethical principles. That is **Grace** in action.*

BODY, MIND and SOUL

The relationship between the body, the mind and the soul has been a topic of conversation for many centuries. For just about everyone it is obvious we have a body. For most it is clear we have a mind. Materialists understand the mind to be the same as the brain, but the word "mind" is a philosophical term more than it is a synonym for the brain. Religious people see the mind as more than the brain, more than electrical circuits and organic cells. The jury is still out on a scientific explanation of exactly what comprises the brain. The brain has been the subject of years of scientific research and inquiry, yet still has abilities not explained by a physiological explanation.

The soul appears to be in a class of its own. Ignored by most scientists as metaphor and myth, the soul nevertheless occupies a central place at most religious tables of serious conversation. The soul is viewed by Western religionists as eternal, vacating the body upon death to move to other conditions in keeping with a person's life and beliefs. The body returns to the elements out of which it came. Most secularists hold the mind or brain to dissipate it's energy and simply degenerate into more basic organic components as the body is prone to do.

To quote a song from the sixties: "Is that all there is?" Many people believe not. While there is no clearly defined reason to suppose the material view of reality is shortsighted, one appears unable to prove otherwise.

There is a way of understanding Body, Mind and Soul that may satisfy both Religion and Science, once one lets go of theological holdings and rigid traditional scientific methods. It is not unique to this book. It has been expressed in different terms by modern metaphysicians and ancient philosophers still held in high regard. It draws on old and modern concepts devised by thoughtful historic figures either unaware of modern secular science or adding a new voice in the presence of strict scientific experimentation. It jumps with dexterity from concept to conclusion because it has already been a part of various conclusions previously drawn.

To understand the soul apart from God is impossible. The two are linked, not only by outcome, but also by origin. Understanding God as both all and nothing, helps set the stage for understanding the place of the soul in a real world still filled with anomalies and discoveries. Let's start with understanding God in God's primordial state as nothingness itself. Nothingness is infinite in a four dimensional universe. Nothingness under-girds what is, as the sea under-girds what travels through it. It is the ultimate medium that instruments can't detect because there is nothing to detect. It weighs nothing, cannot be seen as such and is not restricted to time or location. Nothingness is God's form. But God's nothingness is not how we typically think of it. Divine nothingness has total consciousness, total intelligence, and total awareness. Divine nothingness also has the capability of producing something; in fact, an infinite number of somethings to fill space.

God as nothing fulfills Father Augustine's maxim: God created out of nothing, "Ex Nihilo." Indeed God was before creation because God was the nothingness out of which everything came into being. The writer of the Tao Te Ching nails it with: "Before there was anything; there was the Tao... The Tao is also everything that is." The writer confesses that he does not know what to call it so he calls it Tao. We could say, the short word, God, will do. Western Christianity likes the word Spirit, a word coming out of Greek thought and language. Hebrews describe God in more active terms such as Breath or Presence. However we may describe God, we cannot separate God from the proposed identity of man as that which has a soul. Man or humanity becomes a "who" instead of a "what" with the soul.

Mystical Christians, Jews and Moslems further identify man as "a" or "the" "Spark of Divinity." Kabbalistic Jews say we all have the Spark of Divinity within us. Eastern Hindus say we all have the divine Atman within us, traveling within us lifetime after lifetime until released into the totality of Brahman when all negativity has gone and the soul is ready to be liberated into the sea of God, disappearing forever. Eastern Buddhists say we carry an aggregate of energy patterns or Skandas that change, reform and draw us back into animal and human life until their energy is spent and the nothingness that remains, can enter the eternal state of Nirvana. Eastern Confucius followers see spirits or souls occupying the heavens or sky eternally, growing into godlike influences over time.

But why would identifying God effect how we identify Man? Because at the heart of man is divine nothingness. The soul is both locational and infinite because it is nothingness within the space we call a living human being. Like God, the Soul is intelligent and aware. In fact, the soul contains all knowledge because the soul is already connected to God out of which it came. Socrates thought so and said so. It is identified as a living soul because it cannot die. It returns to the sea of nothingness that birthed it into humanity and other life forms. Yes, animals have souls and thus in their essence, go to a condition between lifetimes awaiting us. But animals are pre humans evolving lifetimes to become human. As humans, their ultimate destiny changes from creation to totality.

The soul is a co-creator with God, as man was born to be a co-creator with God. As God created, and creates, out of nothing, so the soul creates a living series of shells surrounding it that locate it in time and space. The outermost shell is the body, the final generation of the soul's creation and the one making direct contact with this four dimensional reality we call the world. Inner shells include an astral body that has both form and recognizable patterns. Inward from the astral body is the soul body that appears as a spark. The astral body occupies the physical house of the soul and can travel in a dimension that interacts with the four dimensional physical reality of our world. The astral body leaves with our soul upon death and can continue through incarnated lifetimes or reside comfortably in an invisible condition with other astral bodies.

As a composite of mind, body and soul we continue to generate elements of creation. We have the freedom to create because that which is god within, our soul, has the same capability as the eternal God. The entire process of generation or evolution is the process of creating out of nothing. Freedom of choice has its origin in nothingness and freedom of choice is freedom to grow, evolve and become full inheritors with God. That translates into freedom to make mistakes, make amends and repent of wrong actions and intentions we may have taken. That also translates into our ability to change our circumstances, obtain our heart's desire and enjoy activities new to our past experience. We have freedom because we have a central part of our composite being that is essentially nothingness and nothingness is the seedbed of all creation.

Freedom travels throughout our composite bodies. Our mental body, once liberated from past negative and limiting thinking, can generate positive impulses which become physical reality as we are drawn to envision them in physical time and space. Our astral body, once liberated from believing it is the physical body, is able to travel at will. But astral travel, as it is known by adepts and mystics, requires a note of caution. The astral body is attached to the physical body by a thin energy cord. If snapped or broken, the astral body will not return to its host and the physical body will die. A thin cord attaches each body to the other. The cord is the conduit of creational change and normally withers when we die. At death, energy no longer flows from the soul and astral form into the physical body.

The purpose of having a life here involves several key elements. First, we are born into this life to fulfill our wish to experience particularized living and all that may entail. Our souls want different and unique experiences that collectively are shared. Those unique moments form an infinitely complex set of varied experiences. They also split into experiences in phase with divine intention and those opposed to divine intention. Experiences against divine intention take on a penultimate life of their own we know as evil. Evil becomes a cohesive energy that continues indefinitely until it is destroyed. Humans create evil by their intentions and deeds. As co-creators with what is eternal, we create evil with every selfish act and selfish desire. We create our ego minds as we develop in this life. The ego mind is not the eternal mind of our soul. It is something created that believes itself to be us. But is not the real us. It is a creation of our experiences. That is why everyone has an ego. Everyone has experiences. A select number of people overcome their ego minds to see reality as it is and God as God is.

The human mind in distinction to the brain, is the cohesive energy pattern which uses the brain. Our developed brains come out of the consciousness we have generated. The initial brain material came with the infant body. The form matrix we were born with generates our physical form with its predispositions; the consciousness matrix we were born with generates our physical brain with its predilections. The Buddha was correct; we bring into each life skandas of consciousness, volition, form, perception and emotion.

The aggregate of interwoven energy that envelops us at birth surrounds our souls. The Buddha remained silent on the matter of the soul's existence, because the nothingness that identifies the soul is best described by silence. The Hindus are also right in saying we all have an eternal soul, indestructible and undefinable, because the nothingness that makes up the soul can neither be destroyed nor defined. It's return to the Godhead is automatic because in a real sense, it never left the Godhead or Totality of God. Western Religions are also correct in identifying the Godhead as personal and humans as having eternal souls, children of this one God. The Godhead has all the positive attributes and intentions we attribute to a personal God. But the Godhead also includes all possibilities, both positive and negative. Otherwise, there would be no possibility of freedom or evolution or growth.

Freedom of choice extends to the soul as well as the interwoven energies the Buddha called skandas. That faction of the planet who developed Western religions, also brought into reality souls that wanted to experience an indefinitely long community of integrated, God intentioned beings who could enjoy community and self awareness. That faction of the planet who developed Eastern religions, also brought into reality souls that wanted to experience an indefinitely long blissful self extinction into the all, some of them call God, some of them call Nirvana and some of them call Tien. Eternal nothingness must allow all options. Two of those options have a long shelf life. The rest recycle back through the beginning to try again.

Noted Ecumenical Christian scholars have wrestled with God's intrinsic nature. Is God personal or impersonal? What does person hood mean anyway? Our side of creation, concerned with particularized expressions, want to understand everything as this and not that, as comparative or superlative. But Western languages, rich in definable nouns, cannot conceive of what is totally pervasive, eternal and infinite. We want to put clothes on God so we can better relate to Him. If God is Nothingness itself and souls are personal expressions of the same nothingness, than God must be both personal and impersonal. God is personal because God can relate directly with our souls, they contain God's DNA, so to speak. God is also personal because our souls have divine intention ready to be realized. The Godhead contains all possibilities but the Godhead doesn't express itself in particularized souls. That part of the Godhead that expresses intention also communicates that intentionality to each soul.

We can relate to what is invisible and infinite because we contain what is both invisible and infinite. That applies to our soul consciousness and to our other qualities that originate in divine intention. We have emotions, wills, perceptions, forms and ego consciousness because divine intention has these qualities raised to an all pervasive degree. God's emotions are love and compassion. God's will is to help us return. God's perceptions see reality as reality. God's forms incarnate at will. God's consciousness is totally aware. God's bliss knows the final outcome and sees that it is good.

All of the major religions recognize the truth of God and the truth of Man, but express it differently. Confucianism recognizes that people need mutual respect, social harmony and peaceful relations if they are to survive and be happy. People also need to respect the will of heaven, their ancestors and the vast array of those occupying Tien (heaven). Buddhism recognizes the impermanence of particulars, things and all material reality. Buddhists also need to release attachments that create unhappy desires that compel them to return in new lifetimes. Hinduism recognizes that people need to change their karmic patterns to positive, selfless patterns in phase with divine intention if they are to unite with what is ultimate. Hindus also recognize that each person carries god within; an expression of what is ultimate, seeking release from the cycle of limitation.

Judaism recognizes that God is One in reality, who offers his intentions through laws and prophets so that people of destiny can live happy, fulfilled lives now and in eternality with the One who gave them his breath. Jews also recognize that divine law allows all societies to discover solutions to problems through respect for God and one another. Christianity recognizes that the God who is all, can choose to incarnate into a human form, transparently reflecting divine will and intention, bidding us to do the same to become a human family of like minded and benevolently intentioned. Christians also recognize the man Jesus as their model and savior, who so perfectly examples God as to open up to us divine destiny.

Islam recognizes that, given human rebellion against God's mandates for right living, all people need to first submit their intentions to the One God by submitting their own wills to the will of Allah first and foremost. Moslems recognize that peace comes to those whose lives are spiritualized by continuous devotion to God and faithful obedience to his will.

Native religions recognize that all life comes from the Great Spirit who manifests through nature, guiding people of the land to respect the land, nature and one another with spiritual reverence and physical acts. Native Americans also recognize their place and part in an ongoing creation story that honors the Great Spirit and all people.

But each religion is also incorrect in what it proposes when it substitutes its original call with doctrinal, dogmatic, and theological positions. Theological positions amplify doctrines and move away from the truth that came with the original message. Exclusive claims separate humanity into us and them, dividing us from them and planting the seeds of conflict and hate. Dogmatic positions come with power and control. They create helplessness and oppression in their wake. Those feeling helpless, offer their own dogmatic solutions, generating death and suffering in the name of ideology.

The waning imperial power of Rome transferred to the Byzantium Christian Empire, creating an authoritarian system that did not allow other beliefs. The Roman Catholic Church broke off, creating two authoritarian belief systems which both condemned variations not in keeping with church doctrine.

With the rise of Constantine's power, power was transferred to the Christian bishops who quickly consolidated their own theological holdings to make Christ Jesus the only begotten son of God and the Church the only way to salvation. Jewish understandings and influence were forgotten in centuries of anti-Semitism and social persecution.

With the Roman position of "the power of the Keys" given through Peter to the Bishops of Rome, salvation through belief in Jesus as Christ was posited in the Church, the recognized Body of Christ on earth. Transfer was complete. Jesus the Messiah of Israel became the Cosmic Christ for all nations. Salvation moved from practicing the Law given by Moses to the people, to practicing the approved teachings of Mother Church in compliance with tradition, approved doctrine and pronouncements of the Holy Father in Rome, the Pope. Judaism, the root of Christianity, became an Old Testament, replaced by a people driven organization. What was divinely instituted on Mount Sinai became the province of the Apostolic Party now ensconced in Rome. Orthodoxy, believing correctly, transferred to Catholicism, believing what was pronounced as universally true for all time. Since the time of the Emperor Constantine, the Church has not liked or condoned pluralism. Pluralism found its way back with the Protestant Reformation. One of the central propositions of the reformers was freedom of conscience to believe as you felt it to be true, using the Bible as your guide. Multiple denominations would arise from this single proposition continuing to the present day.

After the several severe wars in Europe following the Reformation, Europeans finally decided to accept one another's differences. But even here the differences accepted belonged to the churches that had power. Beliefs systems with little or no power were persecuted as heretical and not in compliance with the public good. Michael Servetus was burned at the stake for promoting his Unitarian belief. Swiss Brethren and Mennonites were beaten and driven out of communities that gave them birth. National interests supported several churches but not all. The New World provided sanctuary for those dissident groups seeking a non-ideological conscientious driven faith. In time, other expressions would be accepted.

Christianity has always had trouble with power since its beginnings during the height of the Roman Empire. Islam has had a similar issue with power since the second rightly guided caliphate. Spreading the faith of Islam brought with it forced conversions, something specifically outlawed in the Holy Qur'an. The prophet himself never compelled anyone to be a submissive follower of Allah, yet with power historic leaders of Islam have done what Christian leaders have done, driven over the helpless for their own good. Judaism has never done that, perhaps because it knows full well the oppressor's boot. Buddhism has never done so, because doing so would severely jeopardize reaching enlightenment. Hinduism has never done so, though the Mauryan empire's greatest conqueror, King Asoka, caused many to die in his quest for land. But Hinduism cannot do what negates union with God, namely oppression.

How does the history of both Christianity and Islam effect the nature of the Body, Mind and Soul? Simply because both religions, while speaking about spiritual issues, have relegated them to a place below doctrinal and traditional requirements. When the body is regarded as something to be punished or sacrificed, it is not understood as the extension of the soul, but a house easily discarded. When the ego mind is regarded as something to be converted, it is not understood as something to be made transparent. When the soul is regarded as something to be snatched from hell and damnation, it is not regarded as something to be awakened. How many more centuries will it take of unnecessary pain and suffering before the Western religions of Christianity and Islam awaken to realize salvation comes from within, the personal and social result of inquiry, ethical attitudes and awakened consciousness?

The body is spoken of in the Christian New Testament as the Temple for the Holy Spirit. It is indeed the Temple housing that which in essence is nothingness, yet has been created by God through the god within to act as that which is holy and worthy of respect. The body therefore needs wholeness to operate at optimal effectiveness and live to realize its full spiritual potential. It does not accomplish its end by sacrificing itself for a military or religious cause or putting itself in unnecessary harm's way, but by applying all means of healing and wholeness and peace to its daily regiment. Healing is the birthright of humans. Wholeness is the goal of humanity on both the individual and societal level.

The astral body, a complex of skandas or aggregates of generated energy, lives within the outline of the body. For Buddhists, the body's skandas are to be transformed to the point of extinction. For Hindus, the astral body is to be transformed through rigorous discipline to give up selfish and shortsighted perceptions to realize its kinship with what is internally eternal. For Confucianists, the astral body is present to aide the person to harmonize with society. For Jews, the astral body provides evidence of God's breath and thus should be honored as worthy of righteous living in keeping with God's given commandments. For Christians, the astral body emanates spiritual values identifying persons as saintly or evil. For Moslems, particularly Sufis, the astral body is a mode of transportation to heavenly conditions.

The astral body goes to a condition in keeping with a person's life and inner intentions. Those who have tried to live a good life or tried to be faithful to the ideals of their religious teachings or who focus on the central spiritual model of their belief system will be in a condition reflective of what they anticipate. The soul and mental body remain with the soul buried within its shells. The astral, soul and mental bodies are locational and as long as the eternal nothingness we ultimately identify as the soul chooses, will travel from lifetime to lifetime until it is either burned out of its energy and reason for living, or is transformed to a totally integrated state of being, able to enjoy a new heaven and a new earth. Christians, Jews and Moslems ultimately anticipate being with God, as themselves.

In our phenomenal world, ghosts, spirits and aberrations are in fact, astral bodies of deceased persons unable or unwilling to keep going into the condition that is waiting for them. Persons who have met an unfair or unpleasant end are more likely to stay on the earth plane or material dimension looking for justice or resolution to their sudden demise. Persons committed to doing terrible things may discover a way of continuing to do terrible things with unguarded or non-spiritual persons, whose lives invite such intrusions. Generally, guardians representing the eternal nothingness and dedicated to divine intention, intercept, detain or remove such astral bodies to the condition that closely resembles their comfort level and spiritual development. The Church traditionally has called that level, Hell, and such astral bodies devils, jinn or evil spirits.

What lies beyond this plane of existence is multitudinous, multidimensional and amoral in tone. That is why religious people who practice ethical living and trust in a heavenly parent fare better, because they travel to the safety of a benevolent condition peopled by related beings. That is why faith or trust in a higher power counts after your life ends here because it will continue there. The astral body encloses the soul and mental bodies which in turn surround the soul. But all of these are penultimate in nature. Only the soul is ultimately real because it is nothingness itself and cannot be harmed, damaged or destroyed. It returns to the eternal nothingness that birthed it into the existence of time and space.

Practicing spirituality produces minds, bodies and soul bodies that know where they came from and who they belong to. Spiritually minded people practice spirituality. While that may appear obvious, it is initially unrelated to being religious. Practicing religion is external. Practicing spirituality is internal. Spirituality is both the recognition that we are in phase with spiritual intentions and connected to the author of those intentions. To develop spirituality involves practicing the ethical teachings of your religion or ethical teachings in spite of your religion's emphasis. It also involves wanting to be with God or to wanting to be enlightened. Our intention comes from the promptings of our souls what are weary of periodic return, and desire to move forward into a lasting benevolent eternity.

Earlier, we discussed the reason we want to come into this life. The second reason follows the first one of wanting to experience choices. It is to discover ourselves as God's elect, children freely coming home via a path of diverse moments. We cannot know God without a free consciousness able to negate God, disrespect humans or selfishly follow a self destructive path. That which is beyond time and space knows every outcome but has chosen not to challenge individual outcomes unless asked to rescue, save, deliver or restore those who freely choose their path. Astral bodies or souls coming into each existence have choices reflecting the karma they bring into this life. The soul, fully aware of all choices and their outcomes, chooses which limitations best match a life that leads back to the One who gave it.

Our bodies have senses. Scientists rely on sense perception and instruments that augment sense perception to uncover, discover and otherwise investigate reality. Discovering physical laws and being able to apply them, and design material or electrical devices, is part of that process. Being able to anticipate outcomes is also part of that process. We now have instruments that can detect energy appearances that leave a visible energy trail. Science can never prove the existence of God or the soul, because there is nothing to detect, nothing that can show up on any instrument, nothing that one can experience in any physical way. But science can detect the energy that surrounds the body, colors unseen by normal visible perception, and momentary movements of astral bodies entering this dimension. While such activities are still considered suspect and treated with polite skepticism, more scientific investigators are agreeing that there is something there.

Refined instruments handled by anticipatory researchers will learn more and more about this phenomenal world that interacts with the physical world of material beings and things. The more ethically minded the researchers, the better will be the results. The phenomenal world is meant to be understood, if understanding helps the human condition. Psychics, ghost busters, researchers, exorcists and phenomenologists all can contribute to further identifying shells that enclose the soul, as well as the many manifestations surrounding faith, healing, and wish fulfillment. There is a place that honest, well motivated scientists can meet their counterpart in the religious world.

While the soul itself is nothingness with total awareness, the soul body which encloses it in time and space has memory, intention and intelligence. Some call the soul body by another name, spirit, but it is also identifiable by the description observers have noted when a person dies; namely, a spark of light. The astral body created jointly by the soul body and our experiences, contains what Buddhists call our skandas. It is also known as the ego mind. The ego mind emanates from our mental body which gives it life and awareness. The ego also contains the illusions normal consciousness create. All of this may be confusing until you realize that everything we are and everything we become at any moment, originates in the soul. The soul generates or evolves all of the bodies which serve it while it is choosing to be part of creation.

Mental bodies come from the intrinsic awareness of the soul combining with human experience. They charge the ego mind. Soul bodies come from the intrinsic intention of the soul combining with human experience. They charge the astral body. Form and consciousness also enclose emotions, will and perception, that is, how we understand reality. Each has it role to play, but each also evolves, changes and becomes capable of transformation or disintegration. Transformation includes recognition, repentance and transparency. Disintegration includes letting go of desiring, attachments and taste orientated distinctions. Eastern Spirituality meets Western Spirituality, not in the penultimate outcome, but in the divine intention of ethical living common to both.

Ultimately, all souls disappear into the nothingness of God. Eastern seekers choose the path of all possibilities and no possibilities, through small self annihilation into Brahman or Nirvana, two expressions of one reality. Western seekers choose the path of divine intention and creational fulfillment, through small self transparency and total social integration. Western Heaven or Paradise, is being with God because each is totally with one another in selfless devotion and blissful interaction. God is truly in the midst of such a community because God is realized in each soul aware of the other. Heaven and Paradise last as long as the souls they contain, enjoy the experience of self awareness, happiness, love, mutual respect, justice, peace, integrity and truthfulness. In other words, the community comprising this vast array of witnesses, lasts as long as each soul enjoys the ethical activities of transformed social living.

In time, for time is still measured by Kyros moments, the souls will dissipate their identity and disappear into the all of nothingness. That may be longer than stars exist and a beam of light can traverse the universe and back. At some point, enjoyment is spent and the process can start all over again. The Eastern adepts, having experienced particularized life, opt out of this process by losing their individual identity in favor of the all that is also nothing. Why sign up for being part of a process that doesn't last eternally? Why not? We measure time in years. What has been described as eternity measures time in Kyros moments. When all possible positive moments have been enjoyed, nothingness looks appealing.

All particularities have a shelf life and half life. What is universal does not, because it includes all possibilities. Whatever the particularities are, from stones to energy quanta, from human beings to stars, from memory to volition, from beings of light to gods of evolution, all have a beginning and therefore, an end. What has no beginning also has no end. The soul as a particularized expression within creation carries a soul envelope that has an end. It may last eons, but it has an end. The God who interacts with humans and thus takes on personal qualities began with humans and will end with humans. The God who is nothingness itself didn't begin with humans or any life forms and will not end when all life forms have evolved to their full potential. But since these realities have such a long life span, discussing their end is comparable to discussing the final end of the universe; its that far away.

The half life of radioactive materials is the time period of their radioactivity. Life is infused with God's essence and so God involutes into nature and evolutes through nature, emerging as fully evolved, reaching a final peak. That point metaphorically symbolizes its half life. The other half comprises fulfilled enjoyment. When we realize that everything we consider concrete and real is really symbolic, a creation of momentary perception, we come to realize that reality is process, not eternal things or beings. Change is part of process. Evolution is part of process. Divine intention is part of process designed to aide us to grow up into creationed purpose. God remains all in all, the same yesterday, today and tomorrow.

POLITICS and RELIGIOUS FAITH

American Politics is related to its European cousins, yet has unique qualities that distinguish it from what has gone before and may come later. The historic American scene combines frontier adventure with genteel breeding; freedom of location with ethnic bearing. How the Europeans settled the New World, America, says much of what follows to the present day. Persecuted in Europe for holding certain religious beliefs, many came to these shores to practice their religion without government interference. Many came to own land where they could independently raise families, tend crops and stretch without feeling cramped. Many came to start again, unhappy with the sedentary life they had known. Some came to work off debts. Others were forced to settle here, having been captured as slaves. A mixed population characterizes our Founding period.

Out of this mix two dominant philosophies would emerge. One saw their opportunity in establishing themselves as superior by birth and ability. The other saw their opportunity to establish a rule of equality in spite of surface appearances. One was quick to grasp the advantage of breeding and education. The other wanted to level the playing field for all humans, including the native population, by promoting laws that pertained to all equally. The first saw the place of political influence that weighed on the side of property and finance. The second saw the wisdom of creating a healthy population.

The two basic philosophies finding expression in the two political parties are much older than the American scene. As far back as city states, government systems have supported the singular leadership principle. Great empires have risen from the sands of deserts because a vast number of people have followed one leader. Often, that leader was a god like figure demanding absolute respect and obedience. Often, many rank and file citizens perished to substantiate his greatness and the expansion of his empire.

As far back as the Greek city states, the thought that average citizens were of equal importance, sparked the dream of corporate democratic greatness. Leaders led equally important citizens on quests that all agreed were of national interest. Sparta expressed this type of social philosophy. Athens expressed it in a different way. Decisions were made by consensus, not autocratic commands. But once consensus was pronounced, following leadership then became necessary to effect a successful conclusion.

The first kind of government developed along lines of an elite group who supported a single historic figure who in turn, embodied their values. The single figure delegated functions to the elite and faithful who ruled others right down to the average citizen who in turn knew only to obey or die. The second kind of government developed along lines of a group of mutually respected citizens who honored their tribal leader and what he could offer, without giving up their right to change direction, leadership or designated loyalties.

The first kind of government needed a line of succession or one generation would end its designs of greatness. Royal families seemed to suit this mode of succession. In the case of ancient Egypt, the mode of succession often proved successful since the Pharaohs were considered gods in their own right by virtue of their biological makeup. Being gods, they could rule indefinitely, since gods were meant to rule. In the case of Israel, succession was based on prophesy and prophesy announced the kingly line of David to be the only legitimate succession of leadership. David's line ended with Israel's subjugation, the result of Babylonian conquest. Apocalyptic pronouncements would promise a line of succession that could uncover a leader of supernatural form who would fill the dual role of Israel's Messiah and Israel's king, reigning forever.

The notion that someone should reign predates all societies. The notion that one person is in a unique position to govern others, came into existence with the discovery of power. The Feudal governments that developed throughout Europe, following the demise of the Roman Empire, were made a possibility because of the power Rome demonstrated. Early European feudal societies established lines of succession along genetic criteria, once loyal citizens were convinced that this strain of human leader had both the approval of God and an army ready to be led by such royal breeding. This was not cut and dry, by any means. English history is replete with conspiracies that would determine which royal person could rule, with or without the people's approval.

Feudal systems are not unique to Christian nations. They have developed in other countries as well. Like the Europeans, Islamic countries, rose from tribal groupings, rather than natural boarders. However, Persia, Syria, Assyria, and Egypt were all ancient empires long before Islam came to its boarders. Arabia and Palestine were settled and thriving in their own right prior to Islam formally appearing. Palestine was governed by Byzantium and Arabia by tribal families.

What characterizes a Feudal system is top down management. One chief, Caliph or king surrounded by loyal lieutenants, then govern social layers below him. The number of layers reflects the size and complexity of the people and culture governed. Byzantium presence in all of North Africa followed the Roman Empire's presence that preceded it. Islam easily drove through the Byzantium guard who were ruling on behalf of Constantinople. What is interesting about the relative ease Islam occupied Palestine, Egypt, Syria, Iraq and Iran (Persia) is that the people often welcomed the Islamic forces as liberators. At any rate, they saw little difference to their way of life and were able to accept Islam as their national religion without much soul searching. Part of the reason for this easy transition may be that Christianity offered little social reward for practicing the belief. Part of it may be that Islam, close in time to the life and intentions of the prophet, was reasonable in its demands and tolerant of both Christianity and Judaism within its boarders. Part of it was that, unlike the Roman system of fighting, Islam came swiftly and with determination.

Over centuries of Royal rule and religious intrigue, Europe witnessed numerous wars and societal upheavals. The Twentieth Century would see royal houses fall and a form of Socialism assume the way governments are structured. Social governments have a different character. Governmental bureaucracies run the government and therefore the affairs of society. Civil servants are hired, serve at the mandate of an elected government and generate rules that reflect the elected government's laws. People are ultimately served in a more fair manner than the arbitrary manner of a king or royal governor. The rules are supposed to apply to everyone equally. That is not always the case since relative wealth and social power always find a way to tilt matters in favor of wealth and power.

The transition from royal families to socialism was not that drastic. Royal houses had been forced to give up power to social leaders prior to their abdication. In the Twentieth Century, a number of European countries such as Spain, Holland and England have managed to keep token royal families. Their purpose appears symbolic. Perhaps the royal house reminds the populace of a time of greatness? Perhaps the royal family assumes a similar role to how people in America develop interest in movie stars and sports personalities? Identifying with a royal household, watching and reporting on their goings on, appear to fulfill the same role that movie, television and sports stars are assigned by the Media. They are the rare among the common; the gifted among the average.

The American experiment stands out both for the social structure that finally found acceptance, and for its partial rejection of Socialism. America partially rejected Socialism, but partially accepted socialistic concepts through its labor unions, political party candidates and radical movements. The late Eighteen Hundreds (19th century) would headline radical anarchists around Chicago violently reacting to corporate power. Corporate power in the North Midwest had squeezed the working class to the point of creating a slave caste. Supported by local and federal government, the corporate interests had succeeded in having the anarchists arrested and hanged for crimes they had not committed. The Pullman Strike of that time saw federal troops put down the strike with loss to human life. The coal fields of Northeastern Pennsylvania saw the Molly Maguires kill mine managers as they fought for fair labor conditions and salaries. A Pinkerton agent would testify against the leaders, living to see them hanged in Pottsville. The will of government in a number of instances had spoken and Socialism was dismissed as un-American.

Socialism was the preferred governmental system of Europe. Revolutions had ousted royal households and the people had spoken for a federal system that would both represent them and distribute the nation's wealth to all citizens. Marx and others, saw European Socialism as not going far enough. The class distinctions must go. Communism found it's opportunity to steal a country when Lenin was secretly transported from Germany to Russia to start a revolution.

American style democracy was influenced by the thoughts of such notable social thinkers as John Locke and Jean Jacques Rousseau, whose ideas weighed heavily in the making of the United States Constitution. This constitution constituted a document designed to bypass the parliamentary structures of European governments. Instead of a House of Lords and House of Commons, there were three independent branches formulated to balance one another while acting to regulate the affairs of ordinary citizens. An executive branch was to execute, initiate and direct actions on behalf of the country as a whole. The legislative branch was to enact laws, represent the populace, and regulate revenue. The Judicial branch was to evaluate, enforce and decide on laws passed by legislative bodies according to their legitimate merit, using as its standard the Federal Constitution. Each was to insure the other branches acted in accordance with the best interests of the country and its people as a whole.

Even here the two political/social/financial philosophies had a say. Until the Twentieth century, United States senators were chosen by state legislators and not the people. Revenue followed a capitalistic scheme predicated on moving money and creating incentive to make more money. The political philosophy of the Right, as it would be known, favored the few. The political philosophy of the Left, as it would become known, favored the many. The Right believed and taught that the few knew what was best for the many. The Left believed and taught that the many needed to be protected by government.

The party of privilege has always had an influence consonant with its relative wealth and position. The party of the people has always had an influence consonant with its numbers of working class and immigrant populations. The party of the few has discovered a way of expanding its base. The party of the many has discovered a way of neglecting its base. This new century offers hope that both parties will change or make room for two differently called parties whose relative philosophies will reflect at least fifty percent of the people in every way.

Before there were city states, there were planter cultures living side by side with hunter/gatherer cultures. The planter cultures depended on nature and invisible forces that could either bless or curse their crops. Over time they could build stable cities, learn crafts and invent labor saving devises. They could expand their view past simple survival to explore their world and create new visions. Securing their environment over time afforded them safety and leisure.

The hunter/gatherer cultures practiced a migratory lifestyle depending on game and natural food supplies. They moved around seasonally developing tracking skills and warrior prowess. Being warlike afforded them victories over potential enemies. Survival would become conquest and conquest would bring planter cultures into their orb of influence. But planter cultures seldom dominated their conquering intruders and so patterns of behavior developed that subjugated one element of the population over the other. The dominant party won.

India represents these two groups and their subsequent influence well. Aryan invaders, as hunter/gatherers, entered India interacting with dark Skinned Dasas, whose planter societies had established a sophisticated civilization complete with cities, houses of leisure and gardens of delight. The Aryans dominated the Dasas, blended their own culture with them, and established a ruling class that would direct their movements.

The Aryans were aggressive, self assertive and certain of their relative worth. Their hunting skills taught them to take advantage of prey, subjugate animals and move on when conditions were depleted. The Dasas were gentle, observant and careful of their environment. Their planting skills taught them to depend on forces outside of themselves, live in harmony with their surroundings and appreciate nature, the world and other life forms. Their training also made them easy prey for less psychically evolved but more materially oriented intruders. Before the White Man came to America it was populated by Indians of varying degrees of culture and sophistication. The planter groups found the land to be sustaining, at least for awhile. The hunter/gatherer societies roamed the plains and desert areas following game and seasonal changes. They lived in relative harmony since both types of societies shared the greater land. They also copied from one another. While there were tribes whose reputation made them unpopular, there were tribes whose peaceful ways allowed federations to form and skills to be shared, along with the land.

When the White Man came to these shores things began to change. Europe had been settled. The New World was not. Hunter/gatherer and planter people could not be singled out directly by their relative dispositions and tendencies. The more adventurous hunter types went Westward and Southward. The more planter oriented populations settled in the Northeast and came Westward along the farm belt. The planter type worked at forming treaty relations with the indigenous populations. The hunter type pushed the indigenous populations out, preferring war to mutual cohabitation. In time, the Indians lost their struggle after numerous failed treaties and bloody wars. The planter types suffered but endured in farm country. The hunter types organized along commercial/technical lines, running the railroads, armies and businesses. Commercial interests saw in the Red Man something to be overcome, domesticated and even destroyed. The planter types attempted to respect the Red Man's culture, while romanticizing his plight.

Can we move from making comments about types of people to concepts that organize types into political parties? Making comments draws associations that may or may not fit further scrutiny. Perhaps, it can be done with caution and we can draw concepts from associations, but moving them to conclusions is speculative. Anthropologists have already done this by pointing out racial memory and biological genetic evidence. If Carl Jung was correct and we have racial memory, than those who came from hunter/gatherer societies may still have tendencies that populate current political affiliations.

If those biologists who hold that racial memory is to be found in DNA are correct, then over many thousands of years, we can have tendencies that inform, if not dictate our willingness to follow and prefer one political group over another, as long as we realize that drawing conclusions from data and theory is possible but not conclusive. But let's see how many one to one correlations are available from which a conclusion or two could be drawn?

The conservative element of one political party appears to dictate a philosophy of government that indicates a point of view. What are the characteristics of this point of view?

1) *a utilitarian view of natural resources, including animals, that benefits commercial interests.*

2) *a view that nature is to be used as needed and desired, including animals, forests and manpower.*

3) *a value system that views businesses, corporations and government as the domain of key figures whose wealth and power provide them the right to dictate policy.*

4) *a religious disposition that sees issues as black and white, informed by Christian biblical passages interpreted by clergy who feel comfortable with salvation as other worldly.*

5) *an aggressive winner take all approach founded on being morally right in the face of unethical behavior.*

6) *an ends justifies the means understanding with the prospect of gaining political power, winning the prize and unified social rules of conduct.*

What does the other party value? The party of the people has certainly moved away from the political Left in recent times. Political realties are based on power and control, whichever party is in office. The party of the Left enjoyed the label of Liberal until the party on the Right succeeded in discrediting this identifying symbol. Liberal means freedom and both parties champion freedom.

But the party on the Right champions freedom when it pertains to the ability to make huge amounts of profit. It reflects the hunter who wants to hunt prey and domesticate livestock for utilitarian reasons. Having the right to have guns, and kill game is part of this freedom. The other part is to raise animals, fatten them up by any means, slaughter them by the millions and sell the meat to a population conditioned to eat as much meat as possible. Sales, production, distribution are all hunter activities. Freedom provides them the right to do it according to market conditions and marketing strategies.

The party on the Left champions freedom as well, but their view is individual freedom of choice. Choice pertains to making decisions about where to live, what to do, how to enjoy leisure time, human rights, democratic egalitarian ideals. The party on the Left is more sensitive about environment, animal's rights, conservation of land and wild life. Remembering the benefits of living with nature, the Left sees the whole picture, one planet, establishing balance in the face of Entropy. The Left seeks a steady state economy based on enough for all. The Right prefers infinite growth and damn the torpedoes.

Lets see how these two views may be compared on a one to one basis. What are the characteristics of the Liberal element?

1)   a conservationist view of natural resources, including the humane treatment of all animals.

2)   a view that nature is to be respected and credited for its bounty, with a disposition to sparingly use as needed those resources that are available. The American Indians provide an excellent model for this view.

3)   a value system that views businesses, corporations and government as the domain of the people as a whole, regulated by government as the only strong enough entity able to reign in dishonest, oppressive, depleting, and despoiling examples of corporate greed.

4)   a religious disposition that sees all legitimate religions as having a rightful place at the social/economic table and seeing the role of any authentic religion as worthy of respect. Following the secular model honors the rightful place of each while discounting the claims of some that they have the only way to human salvation.

5)   a populace respect for divergent views founded on a humanitarian view that all people are important and deserving of a place in society and an opportunity to be happy and succeed.

6)   an ethical belief that power should be distributed along lines of native ability and creative contributions. This view holds that what is best for the whole is right.

In the Twentieth Century the elite oriented party began a campaign that would see its representatives holding more and more offices. Its strategy was formulated on several fronts. First, Corporate money supported the one party while also giving less to the other. But corporate money expected a return on its contributions. Second, the elite party turned to conservative social values while remaining faithful to its original view that the few knew what was best for the many. It firmly embraced the conviction that what was best for the few was influence and continued advantage. Advantage is a basic tenant of Business. One sells, owns and grows by having a market and a political advantage. Growth is everything and growth no longer needs to be a byproduct of a better product that benefits more people at a lower cost. Growth is achieved by a legislative body passing laws that make production cheaper even at the expanse of clean air or water. Cheaper production can also be achieved by a friendly relation with large banks who are willing to loan money at a low interest while making it impossible for other businesses to get the same loan.

Third, the commercialization of the Media moved Television and Radio from a service industry for all people to an industry favoring big sponsors willing to pay more money and have more air time to sell their services and views. The vast amounts of political contributions could also be channeled to ads flooding the airways supporting a better financed candidate than a better qualified candidate with little or no money.

The blow to the more populace party came with its decisions to support Gay and Abortion rights. Done in the name of freedom of choice and humanitarian ideals, it went against Christian religious teachings. As several denominations grew with their clear but simplified salvation message, those same denominations railed against what they considered immoral candidate leanings. Murder by abortion trumped the right of a prospective mother to abort an unwanted pregnancy. The moral code championed by the Apostle Paul trumped the humanitarian view that homosexual behavior is no better or worst than heterosexual behavior. More people, both Protestant and Catholic, felt that their Church's teachings and its prohibitions were more important than freedom of choice. Those who promoted Gay rights and allowed abortions were in a distinct, if not militant minority. They would lose their fight.

The Left had counted on separation of Church and State as holding to a secular society that would promote the common good by promoting divergent views. But most people were uncomfortable with a secular society with no moral leanings. Morality is part of this country and part of what it means to be religious. Freedom of religion doesn't mean freedom from religion. The Founding Fathers were religious without being sectarian. That distinction is lost by the Left as they continue on a failed course in the face of social uncertainty and terrorist dangers. Fourth, by railing against secular positions, the conservative element won the loyalties of a large faction of Middle America. Secular resembles and sounds like sex and sin.

Fifth, the conservative element would finally promote a close identification with morality and not money. Money and wealth had characterized the politically conservative element. Their ability to throw millions of dollars around had been checked by large unions whose contributions to the Left had leveled the playing field. Years of conservative administrations had weakened the large unions and disabled the union movement. Those contributions would dry up. The Left would need the help of large corporate contributions and these came with a price. Conservative churches, often known as Evangelicals, Fundamentalist, and non-Denominational, sided with the party they felt held up their few but powerful values. Large churches of this kind could marshall large bodies of votes. Religious power was handed over to political power.

There are ethical and moral values in each and all religions. Studying the teachings and scriptures of different religions alerts one to how little is said of gay life styles and abortion. Most ethical teachings and moral values pertain to how one treats others. This includes Christian and Jewish teachings and scriptures. Both teach against falsehood, greed, oppressive behavior, killing people (not just infants), and taking what is not yours. Both encourage compassion, love, forgiveness, truthfulness, generosity to all, equal treatment of all and sharing with those in need. These values were present in the party on the Left but not pronounced as religious. The party on the Right knows about them, but its preachers and priests seem to have forgotten their relative worth.

The two political philosophies began some time before the American Revolution. They may have even begun much earlier at the time of Hunter/Gatherer and planter societies. They do appear to reflect attitudinal qualities. At one point, high church groups favored the elite party because many of its members came from the upper class. Churches that held both high and low liturgies represented a mix of elite and populace political affiliations consonant with their church practices. But in the Twentieth Century, the growing Fundamentalist and non-denominational churches, who had carefully steered away from political involvement in the early half of that century, began to show a preference for conservative social politics.

Holding the Bible to be the inerrant Word of God contributed to their involvement. Understanding politicians and the political process to be corrupt kept them out of any involvement. With the election of a conservative president who publicly professed a Christian disposition, the Born-Again Christians saw some ray of hope in transforming the process. Once they were identified by the Right as representing a potential block of votes, the wooing began in earnest. The Left had wooed the high liturgical Christians with some success. First the bishops became liberal, then the pastors and priests followed and finally the upper class rank and file worshippers. It was a top down approach. The old money people felt a need to be generous to meet the needs of the poor. The new money people preferred the aggressive influence of corporations and big businesses in politics and stayed away.

Wooing the Fundamentalists and Evangelicals who prized their social independence could not be done with bribery. It had to be done by initiating moral language in the political discourse. President elect Jimmy Carter had succeeded in doing just that and his election awakened in the Right the need to tap this rich resource. When President elect Ronald Reagan demonstrated both a moral tone and a strong leadership personality, the best combination appeared. Carter's inability to bring the hostages back from Iran hurt him in that pivotal election. Reagan's behind the scene's ability to negotiate for their release demonstrated that a strong persona counts for much.

It is no accident the present conservative Right has been able to consolidate corporate money people, conservatives and a Religious Middle America who abhor immorality and secular values. It is no accident the liberal Left, set in a trench of past glory can't see the signs that would discredit their candidates. It will take a people party unimpressed with media pundits and their effete analyses, to convince the greater number of honest and hardworking citizens that any elite political party that favors big anything is not good for their personal and family welfare. Since it will take a truly nonpolitical person; a system where money is not crucial to run for national office; and a national media that will stay out of instant analysis of words, it seems unlikely the national political scene will soon change. Money controls politics, government, media, religion, and the market place. What can change that fact of life?

Faith is a word that includes much more than religion. In fact, there are religions that don't believe in the value of faith. Martin Luther brought this word to religious prominence by assigning it a supreme value. Reverberating the Apostle Paul's words, Luther placed faith at the top of the Christian ladder of moral values. Faith in Jesus offers salvation to all who believe. Faith has also assumed an additional place by representing Christianity. The Faith community is the Christian community of a particular faith. In this context, Faith and Religion refers to Christians who involve themselves in the political process.

In the early part of the Twentieth Century liberal Christians involved themselves in the political process. Laws were changed to protect child labor, corporal punishment in the military and a host of labor mandates to help the working man. Liberal religious figures such as Walter Rauschenbusch championed people caught in social/political conditions not of their own choosing. In the ladder half of the Twentieth Century conservative Christians have also involved themselves in the political process. Laws have been changed to protect corporate interests, the accumulation of wealth, and lower taxes with less services. Present conservative elements are committed to ending abortion rights and gay unions that threaten the family unit. These elements feel that the present cast of elected conservative officials offers them the best hope of overturning liberal laws that frustrate their values. Conservative elements believe that they can control the moral legal climate through solidarity.

But the lesser issues Conservatives are championing will subsume themselves under the greater issues that political and corporate conservatives have denied and compromised. The planet itself will weigh in on this debate of political will and tilt tomorrow's decisions toward simple survival. Global warming, weather changes, earth changes, lack of clean air and water, polluted and overworked oceans and rivers, all will redirect the political discourse away from gay marriages and easy abortions to countless deaths, poverty conditions on a global scale, and a global sense of betrayal.

Nature has to date, not weighed in the debate whether or not taxes should favor the wealthy, resources should be squandered on leisure, persons should be responsible for their fellow man, or animal and plant life should be respected. But that will change, even as terrorists are planning new surprises. They are not immune from the effects of nature. Earthquakes can kill more of them at one time than suicide bombers can over years of needless sacrifice of human life. The two political parties, intent on gaining power, will find themselves in the trenches of their own making. Confucius was right over twenty five centuries ago. The ultimate power rests with heaven, not man. Heaven and its mandate has changed. Forces have been set in motion that words cannot alter. Treat the earth and its life with respect and the earth will return the compliment. Misuse what has been given to you and act counter to divine intention and natural balance, and the results are predictable. Ultimately, it is nature that will decide the outcome.

PERSPECTIVE

*How one see the world forms one's perspective.
Webster's Dictionary defines perspective in a number of ways.
The ones that are used in this chapter and throughout this book
are: "(1) one's mental view of facts, ideas, etc...and their
relationships. And (2) the ability to see all the relevant data in
a meaningful relationship." So one's perspective involves
relationship and relevance. How one sees the world includes
both qualities. How do you see the world and from what point
of view?*

*Relationships are part of living. We form relationships
with other persons, other life forms such as pets, other
institutions such as financial, political and religious and any
number of areas of interest that participate in our lives and
how we choose to live. We have relationship with people, ideas
and events. Our relationships may even be contradictory. We
may like the company of a friend but not agree with that
person's ideas. A particular formative event in our lives may
shape our views yet not effect how we conduct our business on
a daily basis.*

*Relevance pertains to what's important now. It certainly
may include historically important moments that were relevant
at the time but have taken a softer relevance today. A first love
takes on a different tone years later becoming part of our happy
memories but not current interests. Relevance can also pertain
to what is life producing. Ecology is life producing.*

Our present society can be thought of as made up of three groups of people, Liberal, Moderate and Conservative. One could just as easily say: extreme left of center, center, and extreme right of center on issues, be they religious or political or social or even psychological.

Liberal used to mean advocating "Freedom." Exactly what that designation means today is unclear. Our Founding Fathers could be seen as liberal for they fought a revolution to have the right to govern themselves with individual rights of choice. Thomas Jefferson, third president of these United States founded the Democrat/Republican party which managed a number of years until it changed into the Democratic Party with Andrew Jackson. Jefferson certainly believed in freedom of religion, personal rights and populace government. The Democratic Party he actually founded, though not called that, favored the people, leaning on the side of populace ideals. By the Twentieth Century the word on the street was that Democrats favored the working man and therefore unions.

Conservative used to mean advocating "Conservation." Exactly what that designation means today is unclear. Our Founding Fathers could be seen as conservative for they fought a revolution to have the right to conserve their properties, moneys and industries. John Adams, second president of these United States founded the Federalist Party which would become the National Republican Party with John Quincy Adams as their standard bearer. The failure of this Party saw the Wig Party replace them for a season.

The Federalists and then the Whigs were conservative in their views of government and people. This strain felt that educated and cultured people could run the Federal government better than the rabble that could not be trusted with property or money or companies. This Party, with the Industrial Revolution would reform to become the Republican Party with the successful election of Abraham Lincoln. By the Twentieth Century the word on the street was that Republicans favored the large corporations and upper management.

American religion can be described as populace in temperament. The small faction that originally characterized a more conservative element were main line, bishop led. The greater number of people classified as religious were congregation led, democratic in temperament and revival inspired. Episcopalians, Lutherans, Methodists and the Church of the Latter Day Saints organized around bishop pronouncements and upward mobility. Anabaptists, Congregationalists and Independents organized around charismatic preachers and integrated communities. The Civil War fought between the Northern and Southern States would alter Party affiliation in the Twentieth Century. Main line churches, peopled by both conservative and liberally minded congregants would follow their bishops into a liberal orientation that spoke out for civil rights and antipoverty conditions. Congregationally organized churches peopled by simple working folk would follow their older social tradition by reacting to the social changes they grew to resent.

The Democratic led Civil Rights laws would create a political change in the American South. Traditional Democrats would become Republicans. The influx of Industry and Banking Interests in the South would change a rural landscape into a business environment. Businesses favor a conservative environment. During the Civil War, most industries were in the North. That was a determining factor for party affiliation, along with the issue of slavery. In the Twentieth Century, the issue of equal rights, regardless of sex, color or ethnic identity has become a liberal issue. The issue of maintaining traditional religious and social values has become a conservative issue. All of that translates into a conservative reaction to freedom inspired changes that threaten long held beliefs and feelings.

In the Twentieth Century, religion and politics met and formed alliances. Previous values propelled them to organize, but did not mandate them to do so. At the beginning of the Twentieth Century, Congregationalist preachers and activists railed against the inhuman treatment of the large commercial interests that ran the Republican dominated government. Workers were thrown out of their homes by banking foreclosures, large mining, transportation and factory interests forced workers to work under slavery conditions for so little money they couldn't support their families. When Democratic governments took charge, liberally minded religionists petitioned and lobbied them to institute child labor, working condition, minimum wage, and strike laws to level the playing field. Too much power had congregated into too few hands.

In the latter half of the Twentieth Century, the once minority Republican Party, invigorated by a new Republican South, collaborated to launch a strategy that would bring in previously Democratically leaning voters. The first phase was to demean the Liberal label through incessant clever sound bites. Liberals were against victim rights. Liberals, with their politically correct laws, were demoting honest workers to a state of helplessness. Minorities were favored by a liberally inspired government to the detriment of the majority of hardworking laborers. Liberal laws favored the criminal element, creating fear and depression on the part of law abiding citizens. Liberal social programs were giving hard earned money away to persons and families that took without giving back. A liberally minded Congress favored the minority at the expense of the majority of citizens. That wasn't fair.

More recently, the issue of a woman's right to have an abortion, thus killing the growing life within her, prompted Conservative church people, along with a better tuned Republican Party hierarchy, to mandate the rank and file how to vote if they wanted this to end. Never mind, mothers and babies died at the hands of back street abortionists. Killing was wrong, particularly when it involved innocent life. Wars were all right, if the cause was announced as just or justified. Ethical teachings arising from the New Testament were selectively pulled out to justify anti gay lifestyles and abortion happy women who just didn't want that baby. Other ethical teachings were quietly held in confidence as irrelevant.

Well intentioned laws came out of the first part of this pivotal century, but like all laws once put into place, they were not modified to provide for the majority of citizens. Laws are like bulldozers, they run over things and people. Unable to be tweaked, they are finally modified by finding a solution in the voting booth or high court appointments. Passing any law that selectively goes against the religious teachings of a group of voters is at best stupid, and at worst the death knoll of the Party that enacted it. There is nothing wrong with the word or concept of Liberal. But how much freedom should one have before it hurts others. Freedom, according to Chief Justice Oliver Wendell Holmes, is relative. One does not have the right to injure another by what one says or does.

For the same reason, the laws upheld by the Warren Court, a Moderate Republican Court, cannot justify criminal rights if they lead to continued crime. Innocent people need to be proven innocent and released, before they become criminal types by unlawful incarceration. But guilty criminals should not be found innocent by way of technicalities unrelated to their crime. That's common sense, something in short supply for many lawyers. As long as the Court systems are about laws and not justice, they will run the risk of being taken over by populace driven radicals who actually don't care about justice but who do care about victims. It should be difficult to convict a person, but not so difficult, that guilty people go free to do it again. Modern means of proving guilt and innocence need to be mandated for every occasion, not simply high profile cases.

There is nothing wrong with the word or concept of Conservative. To conserve what has lasting value insures the continued life of our species. It also allows society to feel a comfort level with what they feel is right. Our modern age is suffering future shock, the result of too many changes in social norms, priorities and technology. To hold onto what has come up from the past is a good thing. To preserve life, health and well being is a good thing which should not be offset by a person's freedom to do whatever they want. Social norms inform us for a reason. Individual concerns should not offset social concerns. Personal and social issues are part of an organic whole, and laws, political decisions, and law enforcement are all there to serve the public good, not ideologies and vendettas. That is not simply an ideal way of thinking: that is a most practical way of thinking.

The hue and cry of "Separation of Church and State," is perhaps one of the most misunderstood statements to come into the Twenty-First Century. The United States Constitution does not contain that provision. President Thomas Jefferson, writing to a Baptist constituent, wrote about putting a hedge up around the rights of persons to practice their own religion. The Constitution prohibits the government from favoring any religion over another. That has been interpreted as forbidding religious symbols from appearing in public places and religious readings and prayers from being spoken in public schools. That is not what was intended, nor should it ever be mandated that a few can limit what the majority would like to do, see or hear.

The only criteria for any law, legal decision or legislation should be the public good. One criteria for defining a Democracy is the rule of the majority and the rights of the minority. That criteria applies to laws and interpretations of laws. Saying a prayer in a public school doesn't harm anyone who doesn't believe in its content, anymore than a person is harmed who doesn't believe in a commercial moment broadcast into his ears when he wants to hear and see something else. Seeing a religious symbol displayed in a public site doesn't hurt anyone who is of a different persuasion, anymore than seeing that symbol on television. What does hurt many someones is compelling others to believe, accept or otherwise reverence spoken prayers or public symbols if that goes against their own beliefs and conscience. Intelligent and reasonable people already know this. Judges and politicians apparently do not.

Most politicians are not intrinsically honest. They are practical about being elected. Some will not go to any lengths to get elected and some will. Dirty tricks and dishonest campaigning should not be permitted. Whatever a candidate promises should be held to the same standard as taking an oath in a court of law. Candidates who do not fulfill their promises should be removed from office as soon as they do what is different from what he or she pledged. Their administration should be removed at the same time and new elections called. What politicians say is for the faithful who hang on every word and don't care if it is true. That needs to change.

The perspective that works over time is the one that prizes honesty. One need not give away secrets. But any public office needs to be transparent in its intentions and policies. To be otherwise is to invite corruption on a grand scale. A public who rationalizes arrogant positions held by deceitful persons who bluster and bluff, will pay for their loyal political affiliation in years of needless suffering. The world is coming to the point of not having any patience with self seeking, greedily motivated persons and groups who represent Parties and institutions that refuse to act for the greater population in deference to the few who are never satisfied with enough for themselves, even while others live lives of despair.

The perspective that works best over time is the one dedicated to service instead of self seeking. A service attitude helps, lifts, builds trust without promotion, and perpetuates the well being of those being served. The Roman Catholic Church was lifted out of its deteriorating situation by the ideals of a man who came to serve, even as he followed another who came to serve. Saint Francis of Assisi, by selfless acts raised the entire international church of his day to remember the one who came to serve humanity. The lure of money has brought us to the brink of collapse, though the ones committed to promoting money may not realize it. All of our institutions have been corrupted by greed and dishonesty, power and shamelessness. That includes the mega churches whose leadership have created a superficial platform that worships at the feet of a false deity, and ideology in the name of salvation.

The perspective that works over time is the one that practices the ethical teachings found in all the major world religions as well as with secular humanists. Ethical principles bring people together, appreciating what it means to be a community. The get all you can attitude that pervades the competitive model found in all of our social institutions today destroys and damages people, causes and beliefs. Those institutions, such as the Media, have sold out to commercial interests who want the biggest bang for their advertising buck. So they compel television and radio stations to maximize their viewing audience of spenders. Sensationalism trumps meaningful content: clever sound bites trump truthful information: horrific sights trump wise discussions; all for the almighty advertising dollar that pays investors, employees and expenses. That is intrinsically unethical. That is not in keeping with the public good or the Media's mandate to serve public interests. That is crass commercialism, marketing wares to the point of obscenity. That favors big businesses and corporations.

The single goal of any company or corporation is profit. Profit drives companies and corporations to be dishonest, marketing their product or service to hide what is not superior, and emphasize appearance and superficial additions. That single goal drives for power and control, forcing workers to work for less while driving other companies out of business. The driving need to maximize profit encourages greed, while lobbying politicians to look the other way or legislate favorable advantages to large corporations to make even more profit.

The religious perspective that works over time is the one that does not insist on faithful loyalty but truthful discovery. Christians who survive this century, happy in their faith and faithfulness, are those who develop confidence that what they believe and practice is truthful and practical. Subscribing to fear filled loyalty to an institution because the alternative is damnation will find damnation instead of salvation. Salvation brings happiness because it generates positive human relationships and creates trust in what can never be seen but realized in living. Pronouncing the bible as infallible is an indefensible position that separates people of good will and good sense.

The religious perspective that works over time, bringing happiness to its adherers, practices love over hate; joy over certainty; sharing over wealth; justice over advantage; grace over need; and community over self. Realizing happiness is an inner thing independent of holdings, money or social influence. Self actualization is the realization that you have enough because you are enough at each moment. Striving to rise to a condition of perfection while in this body should be relegated to spiritual matters of transparency; not material matters of acquisition and power. Liberal Christians are heading in this direction but won't get to this state until they also are willing to conserve all life, animal, fetal and human. Conservative Christians are heading in this direction but won't get to this state until they also are willing to allow discovery, meaningful change and thus personal transformation.

For all religious people, transparency is the key to social harmony. Jews who practice Torah already are gradually becoming transparent by focusing their consciousness on what is divinely given and spiritually alive. Connecting to Almighty God by hearing his voice in his mitzvahs creates salvation in the now and salvation in the beyond of life. Transparency comes with the God given realization that humanity is to be respected, treated fairly and with compassion. Transparency concludes with the realization that God calls his own as the breather calls back his breath.

Moslems who practice al Qur'an, understanding its spiritual depths, already are gradually becoming transparent by focusing their consciousness on what is divinely given and spiritually alive. Connecting to Allah by selfless obedience to His intentions creates salvation in the now and salvation in the beyond of life. Transparency comes with the God given realization that humanity is to be respected, treated justly and with compassion. Transparency concludes with the felt presence of the All Compassionate One who frees us from the rancor, frustration and revenge minded attitudes so easily carried.

Christians who practice the teachings of Jesus, understanding them as God's plea to create human brotherhood and divine sonship, already are gradually becoming transparent by focusing their activities on selfless acts that bring spiritual life to all. Connecting to one another connects us to God who is in our midst. Transparency comes with a truthful spirit that is set free by that truth.

The Indian Yoga or Buddhist Monk is well on his or her way to being transparent simply by practicing their religion. The Indian Shaman or Taoist priest is well on his or her way to being transparent. The closer we move to what is infinite and all encompassing, the more transparent we become. In time the "me" that is "me" disappears leaving the "all" that is "all." Transparency is the key to happiness whatever religion you practice.

Transparency is the model for all social institutions. Governmental agencies are mandated by legislators to perform a service. The IRS collects rightfully owed taxes so Congress can have money to budget into programs. The Social Security Administration is mandated to collect and issue moneys to recipients deserving by virtue of age or disability. That money has been taken out of earnings so that it can be redistributed to the elderly and infirmed unable to earn more. When Congress borrows from this standing fund and not promptly repays, they are stealing from the people and should be held accountable by the people. Federal enforcement agencies investigate crimes and should be able to do so free of political preferences and interference. Corporations produce a product or service for public consumption. Income received from earnings should be removed to pay good salaries, taxes and investment for future growth and maintenance. Profit should be what's left over, some of which goes to investors and some of which is held in special accounts unable to be touched by anyone, to provide pensions for retired workers. All incomes should be reasonable.

Service sector professions should receive a reasonable income in keeping with the service they provide, not in keeping with all they can earn because they have the power to do so. The cost of medicine is directly related to the monopolistic nature of the profession. Companies that produce drugs, chemical treatments and preventive cures should not be tied to political administrations that protect them from fair pricing and federal oversight. Excessive profits is not the right of any corporation or profession. Excessive profits hurt both the general economy and persons trying to pay their many bills.

Banks and banking interests should be regulated as to how much interest they can charge. A cap of 10% on any credit card or loan should be mandated by a people friendly Congress whose oversight would include banking practices. No matter what credit a customer has, the cap should remain constant, as should the credit amount that is issued. Lower than 10% can be offered on time paying customers, but not more than 10% for any customer. Banks and credit card companies are the reason credit card theft exists. When banks and credit card companies are banned from issuing applications in the mail, and instead require potential customers to personally come into a branch, have their fingerprints taken, voice prints taken, photo and signature verified; credit card thiefs will disappear. Both the Driver's License and bank cards should be blank, containing only a number, electronically marked that only banks can verify. Sales of items using credit or debit card transactions would be verified by a photo electronically sent to the bank.

While it has taken a long time to reach the level of corruption evident today, all social institutions, large privately owned companies, large corporations and Federal Agencies should be held accountable to the public, while simultaneously given an independent status free of interference or manipulation. That would go a long way to correcting the problems. This perspective offers a number of improvements. First, it affords these social entities the opportunity to independently provide service to the larger community served in their domain. Second, it insures honest presentation of the service offered. Third, it insures that whatever service or product offered then benefits all persons effected, not just a few who reap huge profits at the expense of the many. Such a populace approach provides the optimal environment for a healthy economy and healthy population, that can achieve a level of happiness and independence.

The capitalistic economic system in operation today has encouraged political representatives to access funds they have no right to receive. In the old days that was called bribery, but bribery is hard to prove. Political contributions appear to have the same effect. Contributions from lobbying sources to insure preferential access and favorable legislation, is bribery that hurts the general public good. How to prevent this requires an independent agency to monitor, investigate and prosecute contributions, irregardless of where they originate or to whom they are directed. "Independent" means that top to bottom agency positions do not change with different administrations.

The perspective expressed to this point honors religious orientations that practice ethical principles. It honors, by mandating social and political offices and agencies, a focus on their ability to exist in an ethical and honest fashion. It honors both liberal and conservative principles while favoring the moderate position as preferred. Preferring a moderate position afford flexibility and is not wed to ideolologs who run over ethical principles to access power by Party or association. At the heart of following this perspective, is the hope that we can honestly profess what we believe, practice a humane sort of social interaction and give up enough personal power, so that everyone has access to hope, health and advancement.

We need money to live and appreciate the discoveries our current history has brought us. We don't need to worship acquiring so much money or things as to become materialists. We don't need to impose our morality on others in the name of doing so for their own good. Morality has its own effects, both favorable and unfavorable. Immoral persons suffer from their own choices. As long as their immoral choices don't impact on others, they need the freedom to learn from their choices. Drinking too much, drug addiction, obsessive gambling, cruelty, mean behavior, greediness; in fact, all the traditional vices have their own effects on the people practicing them. Helping them overcome those vices may work. Preventing them from hurting others is required. Preventing criminals from practicing crime is necessary for the public welfare. Balance between expressing freedom and holding values is possible.

The social perspective that works over time encourages free education for all qualified students and free access to food for the elderly and disenfranchised. That idea is as old as the great philosopher Confucius who advocated the same thing twenty-five hundred centuries ago. The alternative is education for the elite and wealthy, and ignorance and poverty for the majority of worthy applicants.

The social perspective that works regards all life forms with respect. We live in an age when hunting for food is unnecessary and killing wild life a cruel sport. In fact, we live in a time when soybeans can be made to taste like any meat we have a desire to eat. Today, we have the capability to produce soybean protein that looks like our favorite meat dish and tastes like that dish. All of the pigs, chicken and beef that are forced to live out their short lives in misery and then butchered by cruel means, is unconscionable. Anyone who has pets and loves animals knows that they have intelligence and feelings, the ability to anticipate and relate. We must reverse our utilitarian attitude toward all life forms, including human beings, and begin treating all life as God would treat the life forms he created. Even if you don't believe in God, you can believe in and practice being a humanitarian. It would incur a cost to stop raising and killing livestock, but it would prompt us to begin living on this planet, respecting the other species that share this planet home with us, and perhaps save humanity from a well deserved extinction. Awareness, laws and penalties begin the process that ends killing for pleasure and taste.

Our Capitalistic system has its parallels in other cultures and societies that also take a utilitarian attitude toward killing animals. Where life is cheap, killing is tolerated. Religion can ameliorate the way killing animals is done. Both Judaism and Islam advocate and even mandate painless killing of animals and only for food, not sport. But our system has taken a page out of the killing War Machine of Nazi Germany. We have made killing cost effective and highly efficient with no regard for the feelings, consciousness or contribution animals make to the continued life of this planet. Cost and profit cloud our minds from any other consideration. After all, Pork Bellies are sold on Wall Street, the bastion of Capitalism. Fortunately, more and more people are becoming sensitive to senseless slaughter and killing, wherever it is practiced. Cruelty and lack of compassion go hand in hand, as do kindness and respect.

Using rather than sharing, characterizes the utilitarian disposition. It is built into the competitive posture of businesses and politics. It is able to lie without flinching, cheat without remorse and destroy without pity. In time, it destroys itself when it breaks down the all important trust society needs, to come together. The utilitarian approach has more recently been witnessed in the many mergers of banks, corporations and agencies. Increased size appears more efficient. The opposite is true. More importantly, increasing corporate size, lays off employees, diminishes service, hurts quality and effects competitive pricing. How does that help the consumer? It doesn't. It helps the few increase profits and claim dividends.

The perspective proposed will be cited as impractical, idealistic, and naive. Oil companies resist stating the effects of burning hydrocarbons on the global environment and thus global warming. Stopping the needless killing of millions of animals will hurt the economy and make consumers angry. All of that clammer will be bandied about by a commercially driven media and press, downplaying long term effects as vague and alarmist. Because the national corporate will is not there; because profit and loss play a significant role in making changes; because the flow of money will shift, all these unrelated reasons will find their way to stop changes that must occur at some point or there will be no future for humanity as we know it. The further you look into the future, the more important it is that changes come now. The more you build on a problem the more the problem creates its own critical mass.

The humanitarian perspective is the best and only one that allows progress, an equitable standard of living and the prospect of social harmony to see us to the Twenty-Second Century. What we don't know or want to know about the balance of nature will bring plagues, epidemics and natural forces that will alter both the natural landscape and society as we know it. Pulling the rubber band until it breaks or flies off to strike a target, insures that all of the ills we as a civilized society have generated will have their deleterious effects. This earth is an organic unit. Reality is an organic unit. Society is an organic unit. Nature is an organic unit. Not learning to live with and respect nature has catastrophic consequences.

Ethical change is possible. Corporations can be encouraged to change their bottom line from profit to service. Governments can change their need for power and control to serving the best interests of all the people. Chemical Industries can change to produce products that don't have negative side effects and for a cost that everyone can afford. Cancer can be unilaterally cured through natural sources, reinstituted into inexpensive body friendly products that activate the body's own immune systems. Oil companies can produce long lasting, heat resistant, nontoxic plastic products. Our energy needs can be met by renewable biodegradable fuels, wind, solar and geothermal sources. The stock market can be reformed to terminate large investors while making available stocks, bonds and certificates to all citizens in proportionate amounts.

Power and wealth can be redistributed, so that both political, economic and social power is shared by most citizens in proportion to their numbers and not their ability to influence legislators. A more populace political and social orientation is both possible and necessary. Animals can be rescued from needless slaughter and substitute foods introduced that taste the same, look the same and have a better effect on human consumption and animal life. The will needs to be there to make these changes. People from all walks of life, wealth and position need to both accept and practice the ethical teachings coming up from a wiser distant past to inform a present out of control moment in human history. The future is indeed now. The means are available. The volition needs to be discovered.

This book and other Books from Fogfree can easily be obtained by going on the Internet and selecting a Book company that sells and distributes books. For example, you can try Barnes & Noble.com or Borders.Com, etc. You may also go to your local book store. If they have an account with Ingram Print, the largest book printer in the U.S.A., they can order any one of these books for you. It may be faster to go on line, but the choice is yours.

Fogfree Books

1) ***Searching for Truths***   by Karl Pohlhaus
   Hard cover- ISBN number- 0-9713823-8-7 $20.00
   Soft cover- ISBN number- 0-9713823-7-9 $10.00

2) ***A View Of Truth from A to Z***   by Karl Pohlhaus
   Hard cover- ISBN number- 0-9713823-1-X $20.00
   Soft Cover- ISBN number- 0-9713823- 0-1 $10.00

3) ***Sacred Roots***   by Rabbi Albert Plotkin
   Hard cover- ISBN number- 0-9713823-2-8 $20.00
   Soft cover- ISBN number- 0-9713823-3-6 $10.00

4) ***New Thought***   by Karl Pohlhaus
   Hard cover- ISBN number-0-9713823-4-4 $20.00
   Soft cover- ISBN number-0-9713823-5-2 $10.00

5) ***Afterlife***   by Karl Pohlhaus
   Hard cover- ISBN number-0-9713823-6-0 $20.00
   Soft cover- ISBN number-0-9713823-9-5 $10.00

6) ***Ethics of World Religions***   by Rabbi Albert Plotkin
   Hard cover-ISBN number- 0-7734-1940-3 $24.00
   Soft cover- ISBN number- 0-9770301-0-5 $12.00

7) ***Spirituality Revisited***   by Karl Pohlhaus
   Hard cover-ISBN number-0-9770301-2-1 $20.00
   Soft cover- ISBN number- 0-9770301-0-5 $10.00

8) ***Comments, Concepts & Conclusions*** by Karl Pohlhaus
   Hard cover-ISBN number-0-9770301-3-X $20.00
   Soft cover- ISBN number-0-9770301-4-8 $10.00

Printed in the United States
41009LVS00001B/27

9 780977 030132